MW01448166

SACHIYO ISHII was born and raised in Japan. She was a money broker on Wall Street and in London before discovering the joy of handicraft after her second son was born. She learned dressmaking and Waldorf doll making and has been designing and creating ever since. She teaches knitting, doll making, wet and dry felting, sewing, crochet and spinning, among other crafts. She has authored a number of best-selling titles for Search Press, selling over 207, 000 books worldwide, and her work regularly appears in knitting magazines. Sachiyo lives in Sussex, UK with her husband and two sons.
Visit her website:
www.knitssachi.com

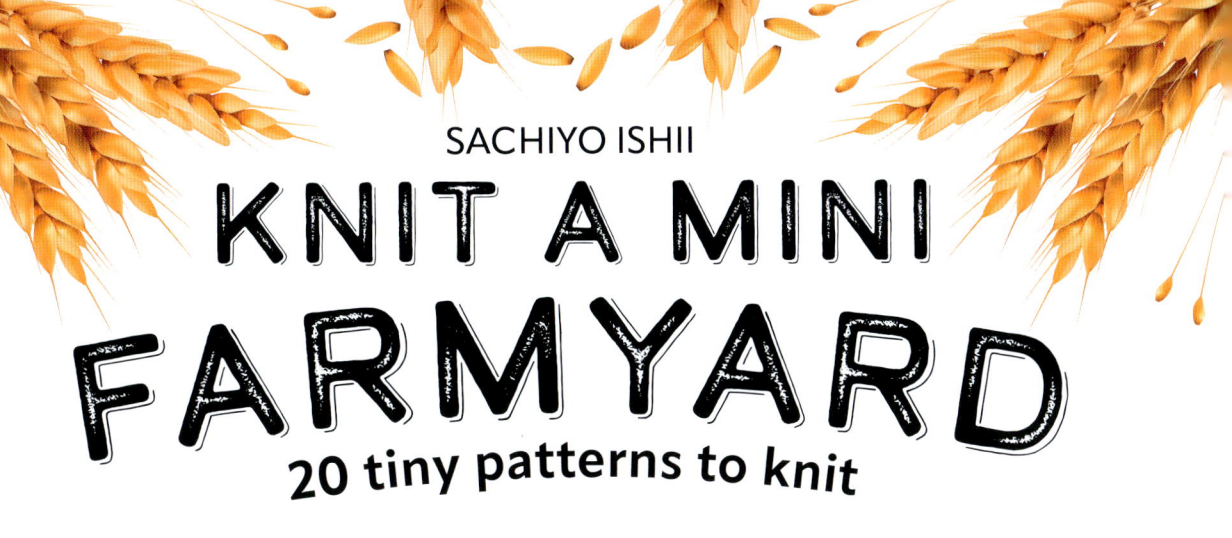

SACHIYO ISHII

KNIT A MINI
FARMYARD

20 tiny patterns to knit

SEARCH PRESS

First published in 2025
This book contains material previously published in
Mini Knitted Farmyard, 2018

Search Press Limited
Wellwood, North Farm Road,
Tunbridge Wells, Kent TN2 3DR

Text copyright © Sachiyo Ishii, 2025
Photographs by Paul Bricknell at Search Press Studios
Photographs and design copyright © Search Press Ltd. 2025

All rights reserved. No part of this book, text, photographs or illustrations may be reproduced or transmitted in any form or by any means by print, photoprint, microfilm, microfiche, photocopier, video, internet or in any way known or as yet unknown, or stored in a retrieval system, without written permission obtained beforehand from Search Press. Printed in China.

ISBN: 978-1-80092-269-3
ebook ISBN: 978-1-80093-268-5

The Publishers and author can accept no responsibility for any consequences arising from the information, advice or instructions given in this publication.

Readers are permitted to reproduce any of the projects in this book for their personal use, or for the purpose of selling for charity, free of charge and without the prior permission of the Publishers. Any use of the items for commercial purposes is not permitted without the prior permission of the Publishers.

Suppliers

If you have difficulty in obtaining any of the materials and equipment mentioned in this book, then please visit the Search Press website for details of suppliers: www.searchpress.com

You are invited to view the author's work at:
– www.etsy.com/shop/sachiyoishii
– her website: www.knitssachi.com
– KnitsbySachi on www.ravelry.com
– Knits by Sachi on Facebook
– @knitsbysachi on Instagram

Join our online crafting community for more farmyard projects by Sachi. Register for free at: www.bookmarkedhub.com

Dedication

This book is dedicated to my dear friend Carol Carey.

Acknowledgements

I would like to thank everyone in the Search Press team, especially Katie French and May Corfield, for helping me to create such a wonderful book. I would also like to thank the designers, Juan Hayward and Emma Sutcliffe, for the beautiful layout and the photographer, Paul Bricknell, for the photography. Thanks also go to Jemima Bicknell for her pattern checking and Clover Mfg Co. Ltd for supplying the tools.

CONTENTS

Introduction 4
Materials and tools 6
Basic knitting 10
Key techniques 12
Sewing up and stuffing 13
Basic embroidery 18

MAKING THE PROJECTS 20

Bull 22
Cow 24
Cat 26
Dog 28
Pony 30
Donkey 32
Alpaca 34

Sheepdog 36
Sheep 38
Pig & piglets 40
Hen & chicks 42
Goat 44
Turkey 46
Pheasant 48

Magpie & crow 50
Scarecrow 52
Pumpkin 56
Vegetables 58
Vegetable patch 60
Fields with pond 62

INTRODUCTION

We came to live in England when my sons were four and six years old. Moving from a big, busy city like Tokyo to a small town in the south of England was a shock, and we had no friends or relatives. We had to start speaking another language. My boys must have found the transition difficult.

I looked out for fun places to visit to keep active young boys busy and soon I found that there were lots of open farmyards nearby. The farmyards had playgrounds, picnic areas and farm shops. We could enjoy pick-your-own fruit, cream teas and ice creams. And we cannot forget about the animals, either. They had a small collection of farm animals, such as goats, pigs, ducks, chickens and ponies.

In my hometown in Japan, most farmers grow rice crops and vegetables. They do not often keep many animals, so these farms were entirely new to me. I enjoyed them as much as the boys did, and this was the place I first encountered the craftsmanship of spinning wool.

To many children, farmyards offer opportunities to meet the animals closely connected to our lives. We read about them, sing about them in songs and draw pictures of them. Some may learn to grow and harvest crops, and to love and nurture animals. I wanted to create this little world with my knitting, and inject my own personality into it.

This was such a fun project to do – a lot of ideas sprang up one after another and I may have got a little carried away! I must admit that not all the items are in proportion; however, I decided that it was fine, since this was my own vision of a farmyard. You can create the projects however you like, though.

You can make one or two of your favourites from the book or make the entire set. It is entirely up to you. You could also turn it into a joint effort as a school or charity project. I hope you have many hours of knitting joy and that the end result is as rewarding for you as it has been for me.

Happy knitting!

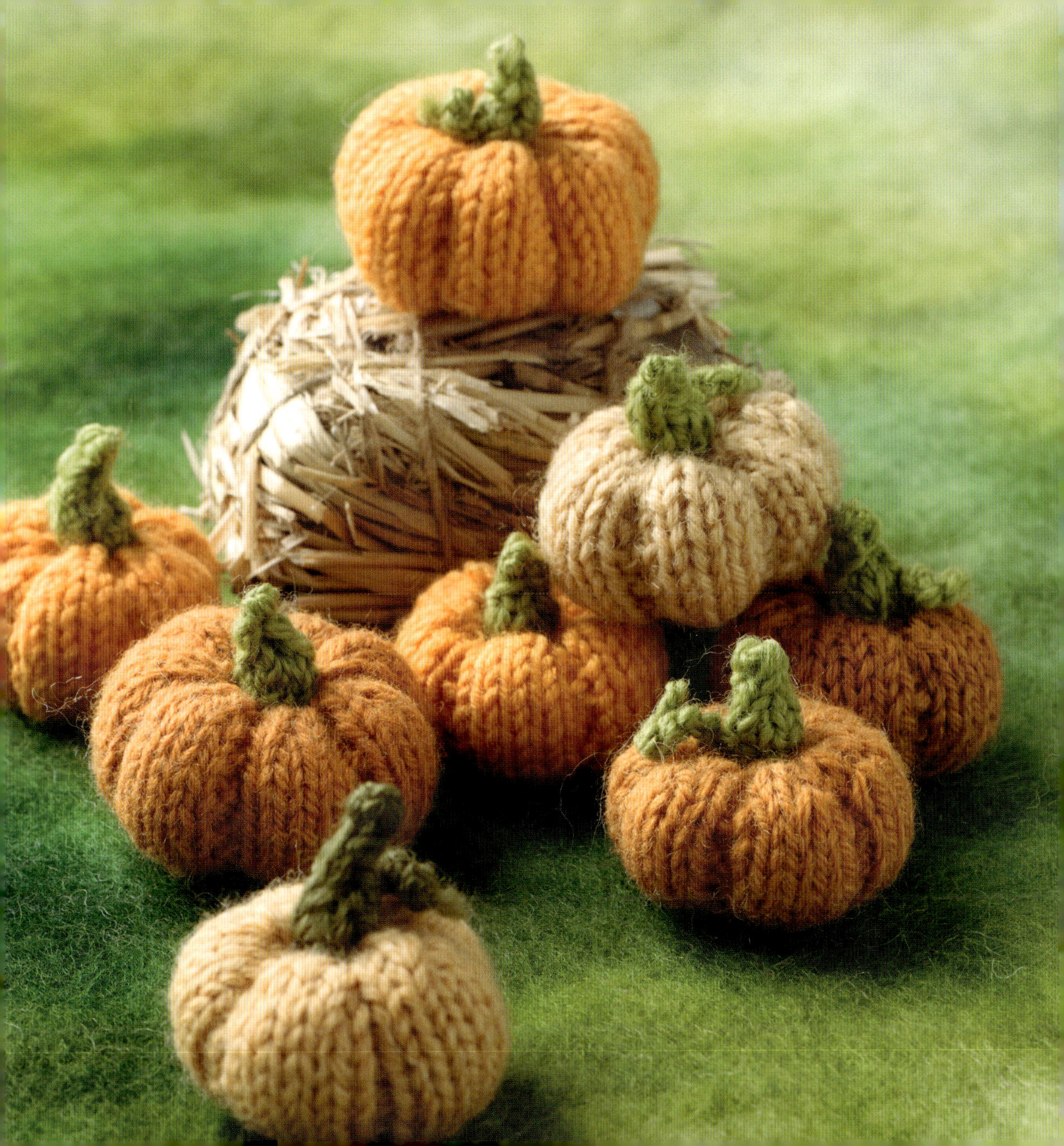

MATERIALS AND TOOLS

Yarn

All the projects in this book are knitted with DK (light worsted/8-ply) yarn. You don't need a lot of yarn to create each animal; the average is about 5g (⅙oz), which is equivalent to a skein of tapestry wool. You may already have oddments of yarn left over from previous projects, so make good use of your stash if you can. When you require more than 4g (⅛oz) for a project the measurement is given in the materials list; less than 4g (⅛oz) and it is simply referred to as 'a small amount'.

I have mainly used 100 per cent wool yarns in the projects, as I love the feel of wool and the colour tones it can create. If you are making animals as children's toys, you might wish to choose natural materials. However, if you are allergic to sheep's wool, choose cotton or synthetic yarns. Tapestry yarn is fairly tightly plied and it gives a clean, finished look. Embroidery or tapestry yarns are an economical choice if you want small quantities of many different colours.

Use 4-ply (fingering) yarn for embroidering faces and body markings. If you do not have any of this, simply separate out a few strands from a length of DK (light worsted/8-ply) yarn.

Stuffing

The farmyard projects are stuffed with uncarded, washed wool fleece. This is ideal for stuffing small toys. It has plenty of bounce, fills the shapes well and reaches right into the tips of small body parts. Some of these wools are naturally brown, which makes them a good choice for filling dark animals.

If you cannot get hold of wool fleece, cotton wool is another good choice. Polyester toy stuffing can be used too, but this can be more difficult to use in small toy parts. For this reason, you could use cotton wool to fill the tips of body parts, then using polyester toy filling to fill the larger parts. Fill the animals a little at a time, teasing the stuffing into place and pushing it right to the tips of the knitted shapes with a chopstick.

Quick guide to washing raw fleece

If you are lucky enough to lay your hands on raw fleece, you can use it for stuffing. It doesn't have to be the top quality. Short hair fleece that isn't suitable for spinning is best, as it has good bounce. However, untreated fleece is very oily and dirty. Here is a quick guide to how to wash it:

- Take a handful of fleece, an amount that will wash comfortably in a bucket.
- Brush off any plant debris.
- Wash the fleece with tepid water a few times.
- Soak it in warm water for a short while with a squirt of washing up liquid or non-expensive shampoo.
- Rinse with tepid water until the water runs clear.
- Put it in a laundry net and spin in your washing machine.
- Spread it out to dry.
- Fluff it out to get rid of any lumps and use it to fill your projects.

Needles

Double-pointed needles size 2.75mm (UK 12, US 2):
This is the needle size I used when creating the farmyard projects. Your knitting tension/gauge needs to be fairly tight, so that when your makes are sewn up the stuffing does not show through between the stitches. If you struggle with knitting DK (light worsted/8-ply) yarn on such fine needles, experiment with larger needles until
you feel more confident. Also remember that synthetic yarn tends to be a bit bulkier than wool types, so this may be another good reason to increase your needle size. I have given a general tension/gauge as a guide on page 9, but tensions/gauges are not specified for any of the projects in this book, as the size of the finished projects doesn't really matter; you can use the same patterns but different yarns to create very different effects. However, if you are making a set of animals, it is a good idea to use the same needle size and yarn weight in order to keep the animals in proportion to each other.

Crochet hook, size 3mm (UK 11, US C/2 or D/3):
A crochet hook is used to make chains and pick up stitches. You do not need to know how to crochet to make the items in this book.

A needle to sew work together: Your animals will be sewn up using the same yarn that you knitted them with – ideally yarn ends if you have left them. I recommend that you use a darning or tapestry needle with a sharp point, as it will be easier to work through your tightly knitted animals than a blunt-ended needle. You can also use the needle for embroidering faces and body parts.

Other materials

Wooden chopsticks: A simple but incredibly effective tool, a chopstick is by far the best instrument for pushing stuffing into your toys. If you don't have one, you could use a large knitting needle or a pencil.
Small scissors: Essential for trimming yarn ends when sewing up.
Craft pliers: This optional but helpful tool can come in handy when you need to pull out a sewing needle from thick layers of knitted pieces.

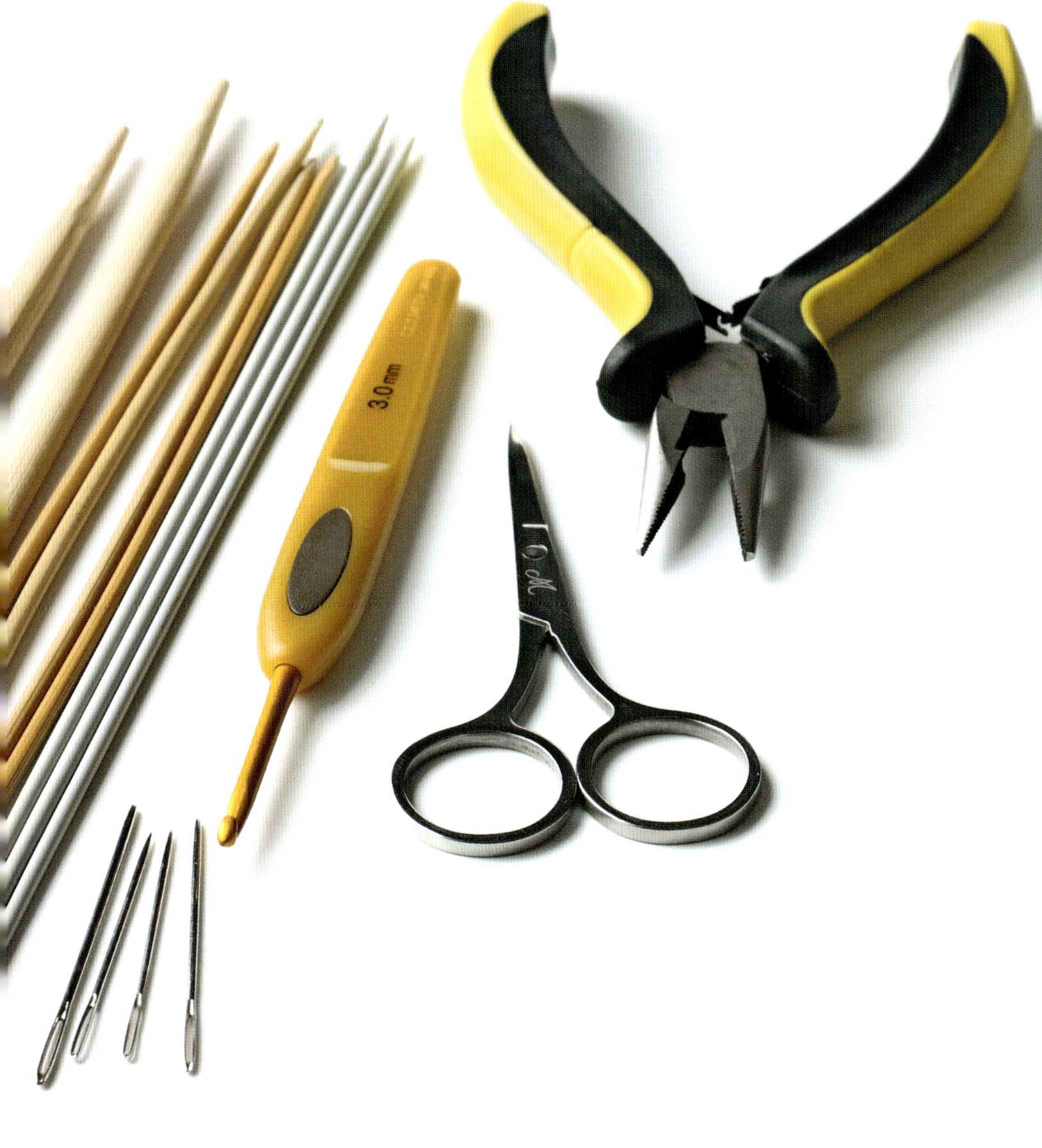
3.0mm

BASIC KNITTING

The stitches used in this book are just very basic knit and purl.
It still amazes me that it is possible to turn small amounts of yarn into something really special using just these two simple techniques.
All the projects are knitted flat with two needles.

Increasing and decreasing
To increase one stitch, knit into the front loop and the back loop of the same stitch.
This will not create a hole, unlike picking up between the stitches or bringing the yarn forward. To decrease one stitch, knit or purl two stitches together.

Yarn ends
Always leave long ends when casting on and fastening off, for sewing up the piece later. Tuck any unsewn yarn ends inside the body of the animal before you sew it up; not only can you reduce waste in this way, but the colour will match and so the stuffing will be less visible.

Tension/gauge
This is only a rough guide and it is not essential to follow it, as long as you keep your own tension/gauge consistent throughout. I work to a tension/gauge of 12 sts and 16 rows over a 4cm (1½in) square, in st/st, using 2.75mm (UK 12, US 2) knitting needles.

> **Tip**
>
> Stretch or rest your hands from time to time if you are not used to knitting tight pieces with small needles. Open and close your hands to exercise them and to avoid them becoming stiff.

Abbreviations

Knitting

beg	begin(ning)
dec	decrease
g-st	garter stitch (knit every row)
inc	increase
k	knit
kf/b	knit into front and back of stitch (increasing one stitch)
k2tog	knit 2 stitches together
p	purl
pf/b	purl into front and back of stitch (increasing one stitch)
p2tog	purl 2 stitches together
RS	right side
skpo	slip 1, knit 1, pass slipped stitch over
sl1	slip 1 stitch
st(s)	stitch(es)
st/st	stocking stitch/ stockinette stitch (knit on right side rows, purl on wrong side rows)
WS	wrong side
yb	bring yarn back
yf	bring yarn forward
yo	yarn over

Crochet

ch	chain

KEY TECHNIQUES

Creating an i-cord
I-cords are used for animal body parts such as the dog's tail (see page 28).

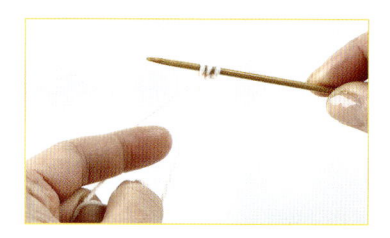

1 Cast on the required number of stitches according to your pattern, using double-pointed needles.

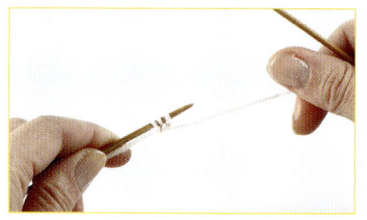

2 Knit one row of stitches, but do not turn your work. Instead, slide the stitches to the other end of the needle. Bring the working yarn behind the stitches and pull tightly.

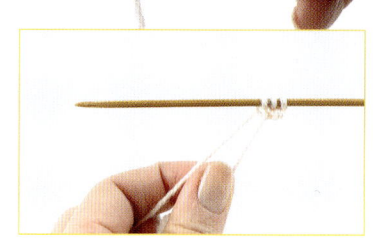

3 Repeat step 2.

4 Continue to repeat step 2 until you have worked the number of rows in your pattern, or until the i-cord reaches the desired length.

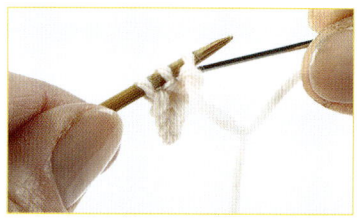

5 Carefully transfer your stitches onto a sewing needle.

6 Take the needle through the last row of stitches a second time.

7 Finish by hiding the yarn ends inside the i-cord.

SEWING UP AND STUFFING

These instructions are for making up animals with long legs. These include the donkey, pony, cow, bull and goat.

The body pieces are tightly knitted, which can sometimes cause the edges to curl up slightly, making them difficult to work with. To create a flat, easy-to-use shape, lay a piece of cloth over the knitted shape and press gently with a steam iron. I have used overcast stitch (see page 19) throughout.

To make up the donkey

Here are the flat pieces for the body and the ears. The edges may curl over a little, so press them gently before you begin (see above).

1 Thread a tapestry needle with the yarn at the cast-on end. Starting with a hind leg, fold the leg in half lengthways and close the tip by working running stitch (see page 18).

2 Using overcast stitch (see page 19), sew along the first hind leg to the top of the leg.

3 At this point, continue your overcast stitches a little further, attaching one of the flaps on the underside of the body in place, in line with the legs.

4 Join in matching yarn at the tip of the other hind leg and repeat steps 1–3 to sew it up. You do not need to knot the yarn end, simply trap the end inside the leg. Your donkey's hind legs should now look like this, with a gap between the two pieces on the underside of the body.

5 Pinch the flaps together on the underside of the body. Using overcast stitch, close the hole between the three edges.

6 This forms the donkey's bottom.

7 Join in new, matching yarn at the tip of one of the front legs and sew along the leg to close it.

8 As in step 3, sew the flap of the underside of the body to the base of the leg.

9 Join in new, matching yarn at the tip of the second front leg and sew along the leg to close it. Also sew the second front flap in place.

10 Using the same piece of yarn, sew from the top of the front legs to the base of the neck.

11 Continue sewing up the donkey's neck and over the top of the head. Tuck in any loose yarn ends before completely closing.

12 The donkey is now ready for stuffing. Push small pieces of stuffing right into the head and along the legs with a chopstick. Tuck in any remaining yarn ends and fill until the animal feels firm.

13 Join in a strand of new, matching yarn and sew the underside closed, from bottom to top, using overcast stitch.

14 For the mane, wind some brown fingering (4-ply) yarn round a piece of card (about the finished width of the mane you require) 100 times, then sew a line along the centre, going over it twice to keep the yarn in place.

15 Cut the loops carefully down each side of the card, then tear the card from the centre sewing line.

16 The mane is now released from the card and ready to attach to the head.

17 Place the mane centrally on the donkey's head and, starting at the bottom, backstitch up the length using matching yarn and fasten off.

18 For the tail, cut brown fingering (4-ply) yarn to 80cm (31½in) and tie the ends together. Double the length three times.

19 With a finger at each end, twist the length of yarn as shown.

20 Insert one end through the other to secure (in the same way you would twist and secure a skein of yarn) and tie the end with another length of yarn.

21 Cut the loops of the tied end and trim. Then position the tail on the back of the donkey and sew it in place using overcast stitch.

22 Thread the yarn end of one ear into your needle and sew it to one side of the head. Use a few stitches to secure it, then fasten off and trim the yarn end. Repeat for the other ear.

23 To create the eyes, bring a strand of fine yarn (or take two strands from a length of DK (light worsted/8-ply yarn) through from the back of the head and out at the front in the position of the first eye, leaving a long tail, then embroider a French knot (see page 18). Take the needle through the head, bringing it out in the position of the second eye and make another French knot.

The finished donkey, sewn up and stuffed.

BASIC EMBROIDERY

Some simple embroidery stitches are used to complete the animals. I most commonly use fingering (4-ply) yarn or two strands taken from DK (light worsted/8-ply) yarn to embroider faces.

Running stitch

This is a probably the simplest embroidery stitch to learn, but is incredibly useful. It is used to create the eyeline for the scarecrow (pages 52–54), to shape the alpaca's back (page 34) and to emphasise the ribbed lines on the pumpkin (page 56).

1 Bring the needle up at A and pull the thread through. Insert the needle at B and bring it up at C. Pull the thread through the fabric.

2 Repeat step 1 to make as many stitches as you wish, making sure that you keep the stitches, and the spaces between them, a regular length.

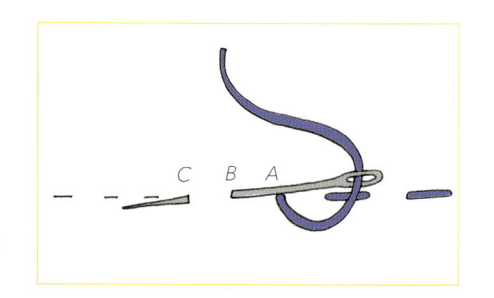

French knots

These are used for most of the characters' eyes. Take the needle through the yarn, separating the fibres, instead of taking the needle out between the stitches. This prevents the eye from sinking into the face.

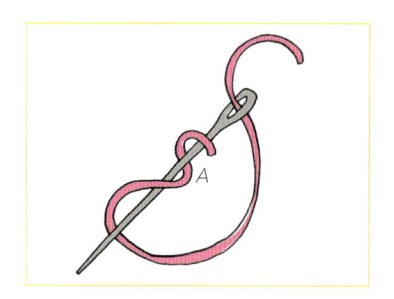

1 Bring the thread through where the knot is required, at A. Holding the thread between your thumb and finger, wrap it around the needle twice.

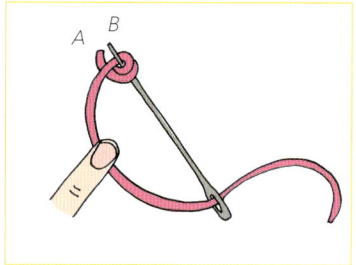

2 Hold the thread firmly with your thumb and turn the needle back to A. Insert it as close to A as possible, at B, and pull the thread through to form a knot.

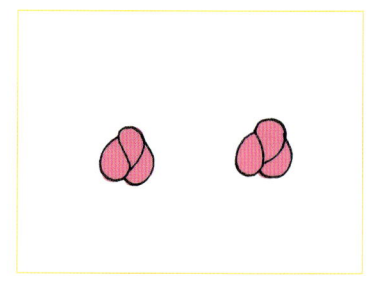

3 Make a small stitch on the wrong side of the fabric before fastening off.

Back stitch

This simple stitch is used to make many features including the cat's nose (page 26), and the goat's beard (page 44).

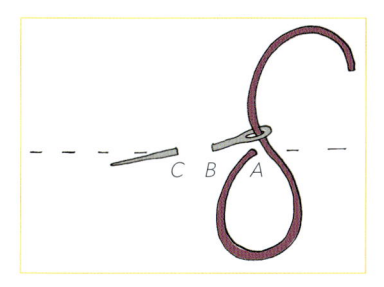

1 Bring the needle up at A and pull the thread through. Insert the needle at B and bring it through at C. Pull the thread through the fabric.

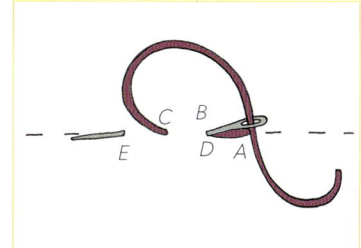

2 Insert the needle at D and bring it up at E. Pull the thread through.

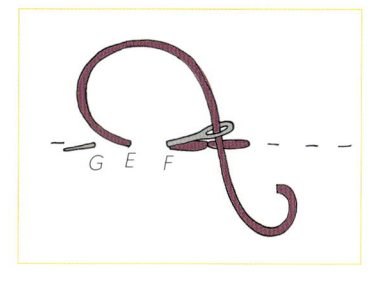

3 Insert the needle at F and bring it up at G. Continue working along the stitch line until it is completed. To finish off, thread your needle through the stitches on the wrong side of your work.

Overcast stitch

Overcast stitch is used to protect the raw edges of knitting or fabric, and sometimes as a decorative element. Another very useful stitch, it is used here mainly for sewing up the legs and bodies of the animals before stuffing them (pages 13–17).

1 Holding both sides of your knitting together, bring the needle from the back to the front, a short way in from the edge and pull the yarn through.

2 Take your needle to the back again and push it through to the front.

3 Repeat this to secure the whole of the edge you are working before fastening off.

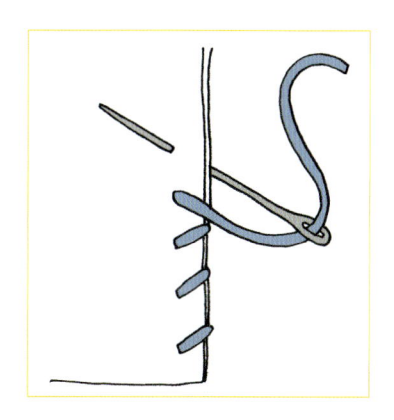

MAKING THE PROJECTS

Bull 22

Cow 24

Cat 26

Dog 28

Pony 30

Donkey 32

Alpaca 34

Sheepdog 36

Sheep 38

Pig & piglets 40

Hen & chicks 42

Goat 44

Turkey 46

Pheasant 48

Magpie & crow 50

Scarecrow 52

Pumpkin 56

Vegetables 58

Vegetable patch 60

Fields with pond 62

BULL

Materials

- 10g (¼oz) of DK (light worsted/8-ply) yarn in red brown (A) and small amounts in off-white (B), gold (C) and dark brown (D)
- Small amount of 4-ply (fingering) yarn in brown (E)
- Stuffing

Additional equipment

3mm (UK 11, US C/2 or D/3) crochet hook

Size

8cm (3¼in) long, 7cm (2¾in) tall

Difficulty level

Intermediate

Instructions

Body

Using yarn A, cast on 35 sts.
Rows 1–7: beg with a k RS row, work 7 rows in st/st.
Row 8: cast off 5 sts, p to end (30 sts).
Row 9: cast off 5 sts, k to end (25 sts).
Row 10: cast on 3 sts, p to end (28 sts).
Row 11: cast on 3 sts, k to end (31 sts).
Rows 12–19: work 8 rows in st/st.
Row 20: cast off 3 sts, p to end (28 sts).
Row 21: cast off 3 sts, k to end (25 sts).
Row 22: cast on 5 sts, p to end (30 sts).
Row 23: cast on 5 sts, k10, kf/b, k3, kf/b, k to end (37 sts).
Row 24: p to end.
Row 25: k6, kf/b, k8, kf/b, k5, kf/b, k8, kf/b, k to end (41 sts).
Rows 26–29: work 4 rows in st/st.
Row 30: cast off 5 sts, p to end (36 sts).
Row 31: cast off 5 sts, k to end (31 sts).
Row 32: cast off 9 sts, p to end (22 sts).
Row 33: cast off 9 sts, k to end (13 sts).
Row 34: cast on 4 sts, p to end (17 sts).
Row 35: cast on 4 sts, k to end (21 sts).
Rows 36–39: work 4 rows in st/st.
Row 40: p2tog, cast off the st on the right needle, cast off all sts to the last 2 sts, p2tog, cast off the last st.

Ears: make two

Using yarn A, cast on 3 sts.
Row 1: p2tog, p1 (2 sts).
Row 2: skpo (1 st).
Fasten off.

Horn

Using yarn B, cast on 2 sts.
Work in i-cord for 8 rows. Pass the first st over the second and fasten off.

Nose ring

Using yarn C and the crochet hook, make 5 ch. Fasten off.

Tail

Using yarn E, make tail (see pages 16–17).

To make up

Referring to the basic animal assembly on pages 13–17, sew the legs. Starting between the front legs, sew the underside of the front body, chin and face. Stuff each leg and the body firmly and close the tummy opening. Sew the ears, horn, tail and nose ring in place. Using yarn D, work a French knot for each eye.

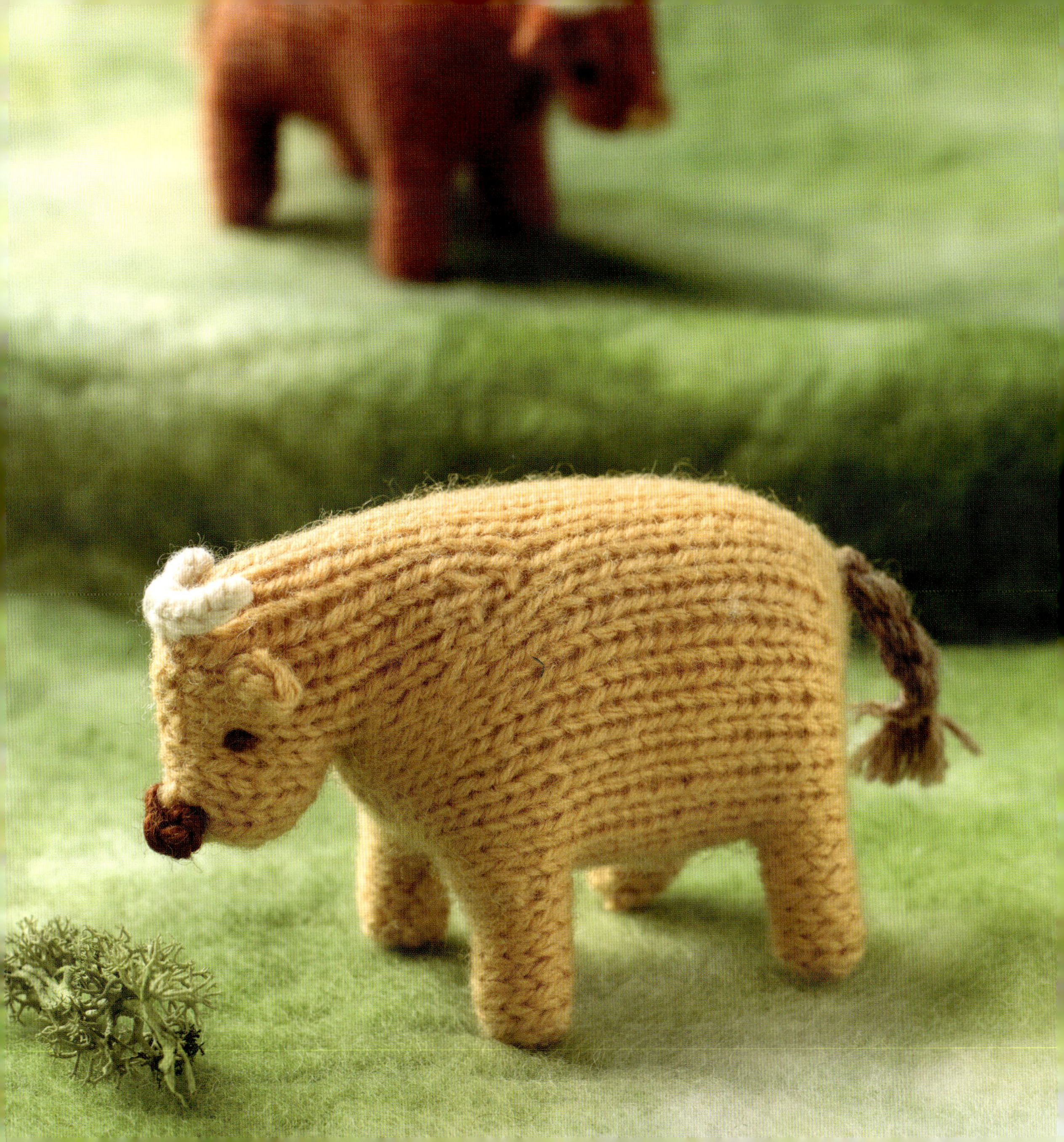

COW

Materials

- 8g (⅕ oz) of DK (light worsted/8-ply) yarn in white (A) and small amounts in black (B), dark brown (D), brown (E) and pale pink (F)
- Small amount of 4-ply (fingering) yarn in light brown (C)
- Stuffing

Additional equipment
3mm (UK 11, US C-2/D-3) crochet hook

Size
8cm (3¼in) long, 7cm (2¾in) tall

Difficulty level
Intermediate

Instructions

Body
Using yarn A, cast on 35 sts.
Work rows 1–22 of chart. Note: the first row of the chart is a RS row; WS rows are read from left to right and RS rows from right to left.
Break yarn B. Using yarn A only, work rows 23–40 as given for the bull (see page 22).

Ears, tail and nose ring
Work given as for the bull, using yarn A for the ears, yarn C for the tail and yarn D for the nose ring.

Horn
Work as given for the bull, using yarn E.

Udder
Using yarn F, cast on 8 sts. Beg with a k RS row, work 14 rows in st/st. Cast off.
Using yarn F, make two large French knots in the centre of the udder piece.

To make up
Make up as given for the bull, using yarn D to work a French knot for each eye. Sew the udder in place.

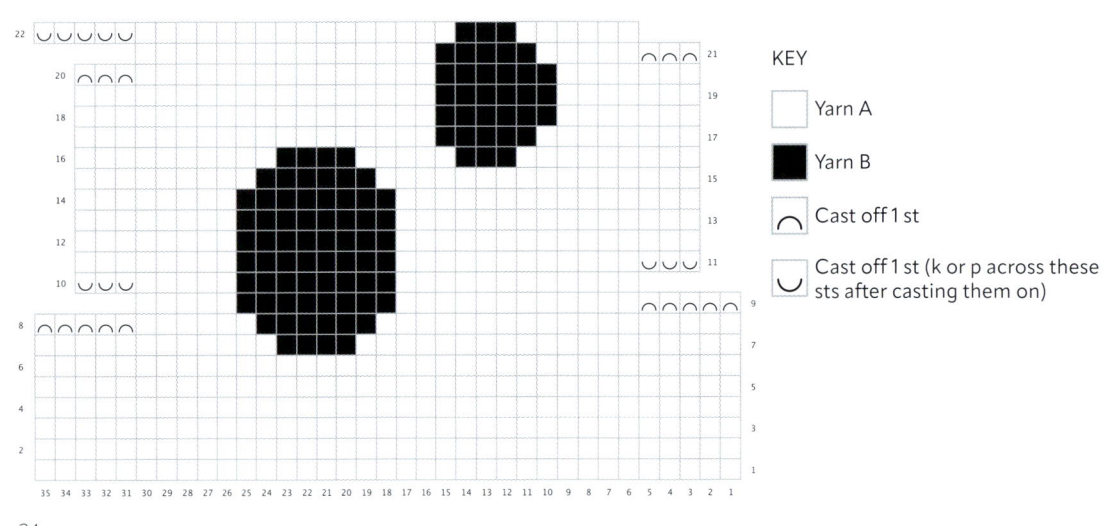

KEY

☐	Yarn A
■	Yarn B
⌒	Cast off 1 st
⌣	Cast off 1 st (k or p across these sts after casting them on)

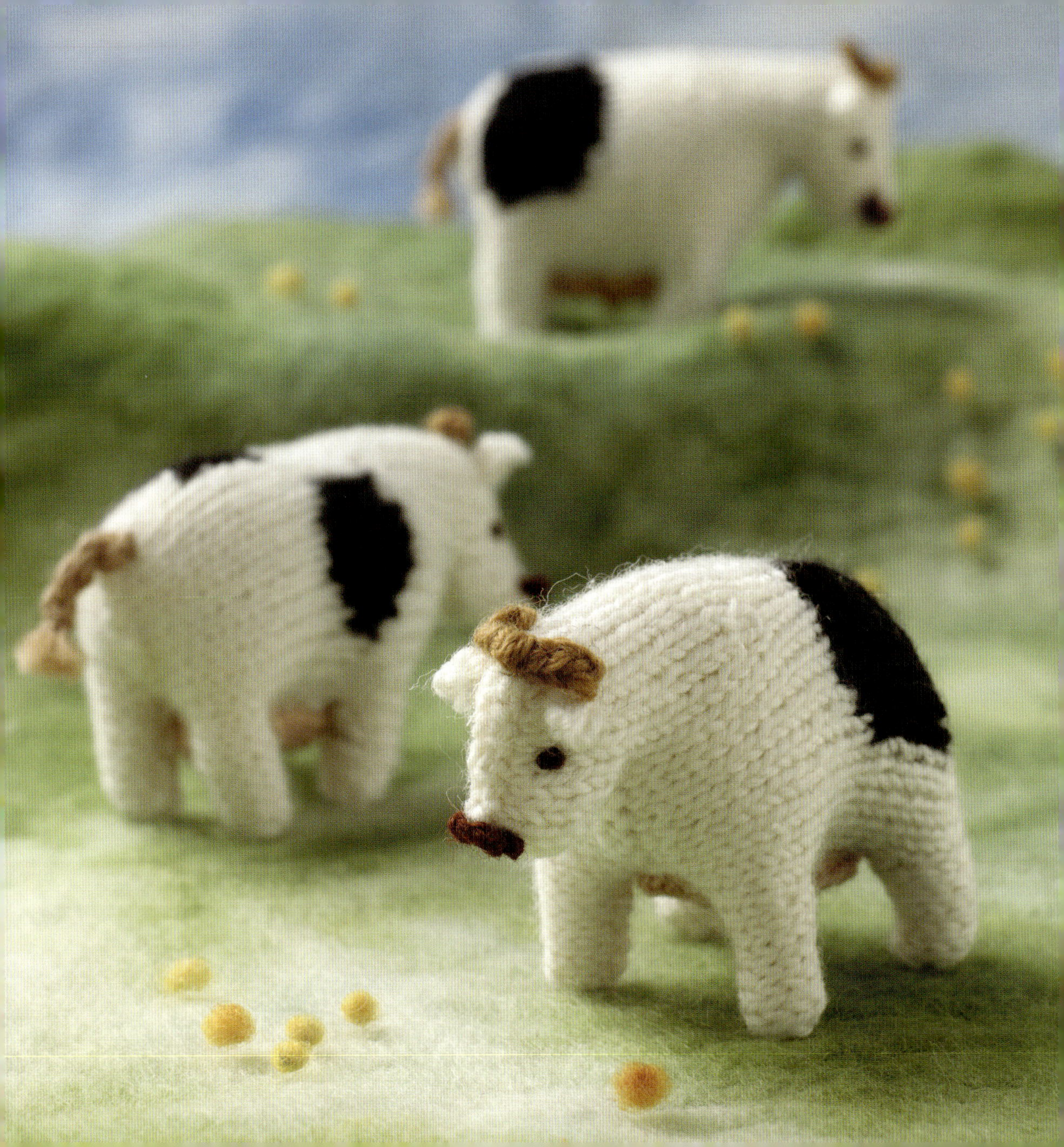

CAT

Materials

- Small amount of DK (light worsted/8-ply) yarn in colour of your choice for the fur (A)
- Small amounts of 4-ply (fingering) yarn in various colours (e.g. dark brown, red brown, light brown or white) for embroidering eyes and whiskers
- Stuffing

Size

4cm (1½in) long

Difficulty level

Intermediate

Instructions

Body

Using yarn A, cast on 13 sts.
Beg with a k RS row, work 18 rows in st/st.
Cast off.

Head

Using yarn A, cast on 12 sts.
Beg with a p WS row, work 6 rows in st/st.
Break yarn and thread through all sts, pull tightly and fasten off.

Tail

Using yarn A, cast on 2 sts.
Work an i-cord for 7 rows.
Fasten off.

Ears: make two

Using yarn A, cast on 3 sts.
Row 1: p1, p2tog (2 sts).
Row 2: skpo (1 st).
Fasten off.

Making up

To create the legs, fold the corners of the body piece in and sew them together with overcast stitch to about 2cm (¾in) from each tip, working towards the centre and leaving a small opening for stuffing through the tummy. Stuff the body from the tummy and close the opening. Seam the head from the fastened-off end, stuff and work running stitch along the cast-on edge to shape the neck. Sew the head onto the body, then sew the ears and tail in place.

Using 4-ply (fingering) yarn in dark brown (or white for black cat), work a French knot for each eye. Using 4-ply (fingering) yarn in dark or light brown, embroider a mouth and nose with short backstitches. Using 4-ply (fingering) yarn in red brown (or white for black cat), embroider three whiskers on each side using short backstitches.

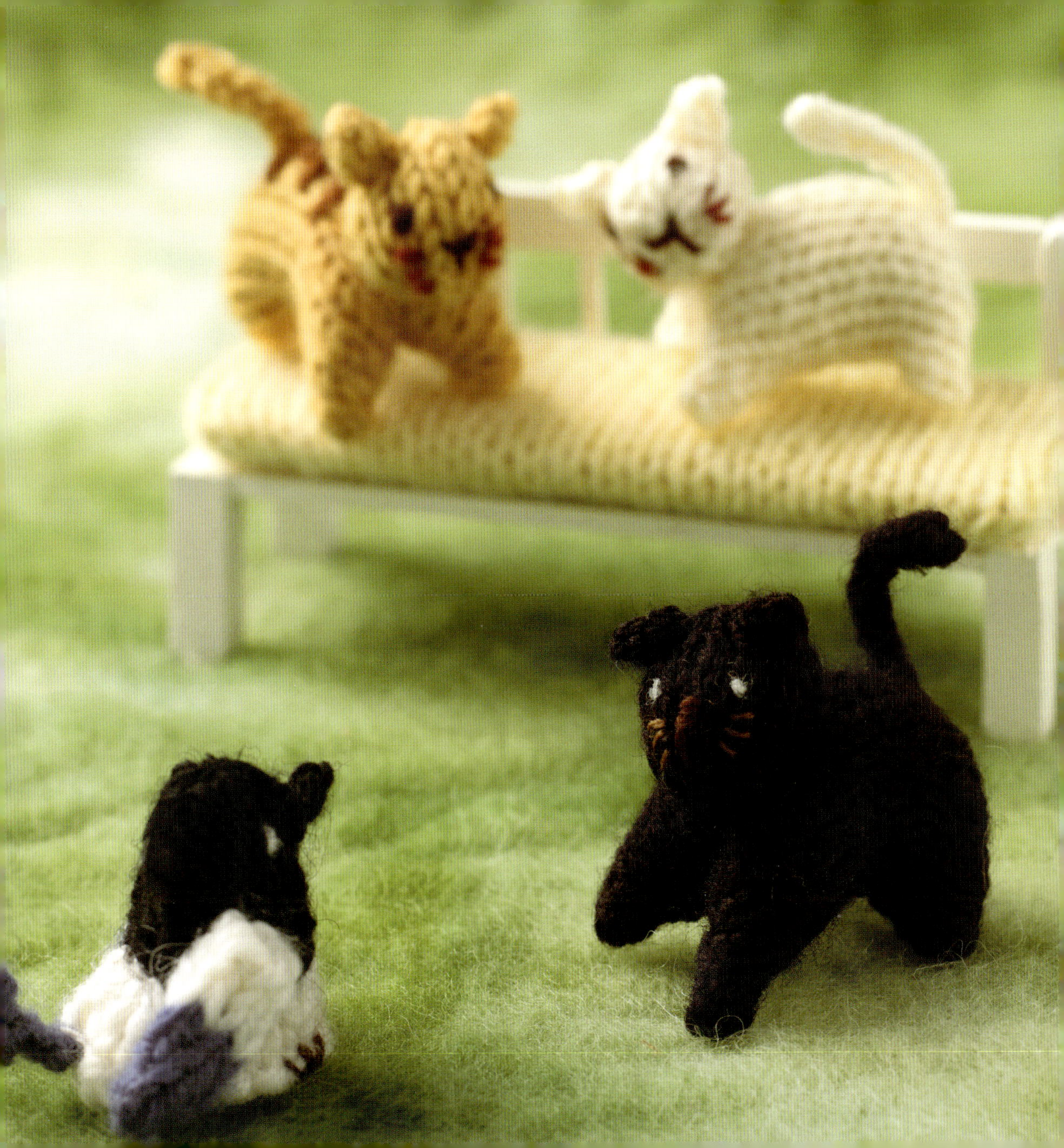

DOG

Materials

- 4g (⅛ oz) of DK (light worsted/ 8-ply) yarn in beige (or fur colour of choice) (A) and small amounts in brown (B), red (C) and dark brown (D)
- Stuffing

Additional equipment

3mm (UK 11, US C/2 or D/3) crochet hook

Size

5cm (2in) long

Difficulty level

Advanced

Instructions

Body and head

Using yarn A, cast on 18 sts.
Rows 1–4: beg with a k RS row, work 4 rows in st/st.
Row 5: cast off 3 sts, k to end (15 sts).
Row 6: cast off 3 sts, p to end (12 sts).
Row 7: cast on 2 sts, k to end (14 sts).
Row 8: cast on 2 sts, p to end (16 sts).
Rows 9 and 10: work 2 rows in st/st.
Row 11: cast off 2 sts, k to end (14 sts).
Row 12: cast off 2 sts, p to end (12 sts).
Row 13: cast on 3 sts, k these 3 sts, k5, (kf/b) twice, k to end (17 sts).
Row 14: cast on 3 sts, p to end (20 sts).
Row 15: k9, (kf/b) twice, k to end (22 sts).
Row 16: p to end.
Row 17: cast off 6 sts, k to end (16 sts).
Row 18: cast off 6 sts, p to end (10 sts).
Row 19: k to end.
Row 20: cast on 3 sts, p to end (13 sts).
Row 21: cast on 3 sts, k to end (16 sts).
Rows 22 and 23: work 2 rows in st/st.
Row 24: p2tog, cast off st on the right needle, cast off all sts to last 2 sts, p2tog, cast off the last st.

Note: the ears and tail are worked in a contrast colour here – alternatively, they may be worked in same colour as the body and head.

Ears: make two

Using yarn B, cast on 3 sts.
Row 1: p to end.
Row 2: skpo, k1 (2 sts).
Row 3: p2tog (1 st).
Fasten off.

Ear variation

For round ears: after cast on, beg with a p WS row, work in st/st for 3 rows. Cast off.

Tail

Using yarn B, cast on 2 sts.
Work an i-cord for 3 rows. Pass the first st over the second and fasten off.

Collar

Using yarn C and crochet hook, make 12 ch.
Fasten off.

To make up

Referring to the basic animal assembly on pages 13–17, sew and stuff the legs and body. Sew the ears, tail and collar in place on the body. Using yarn D, work a French knot for each eye and embroider the nose with short backstitches.

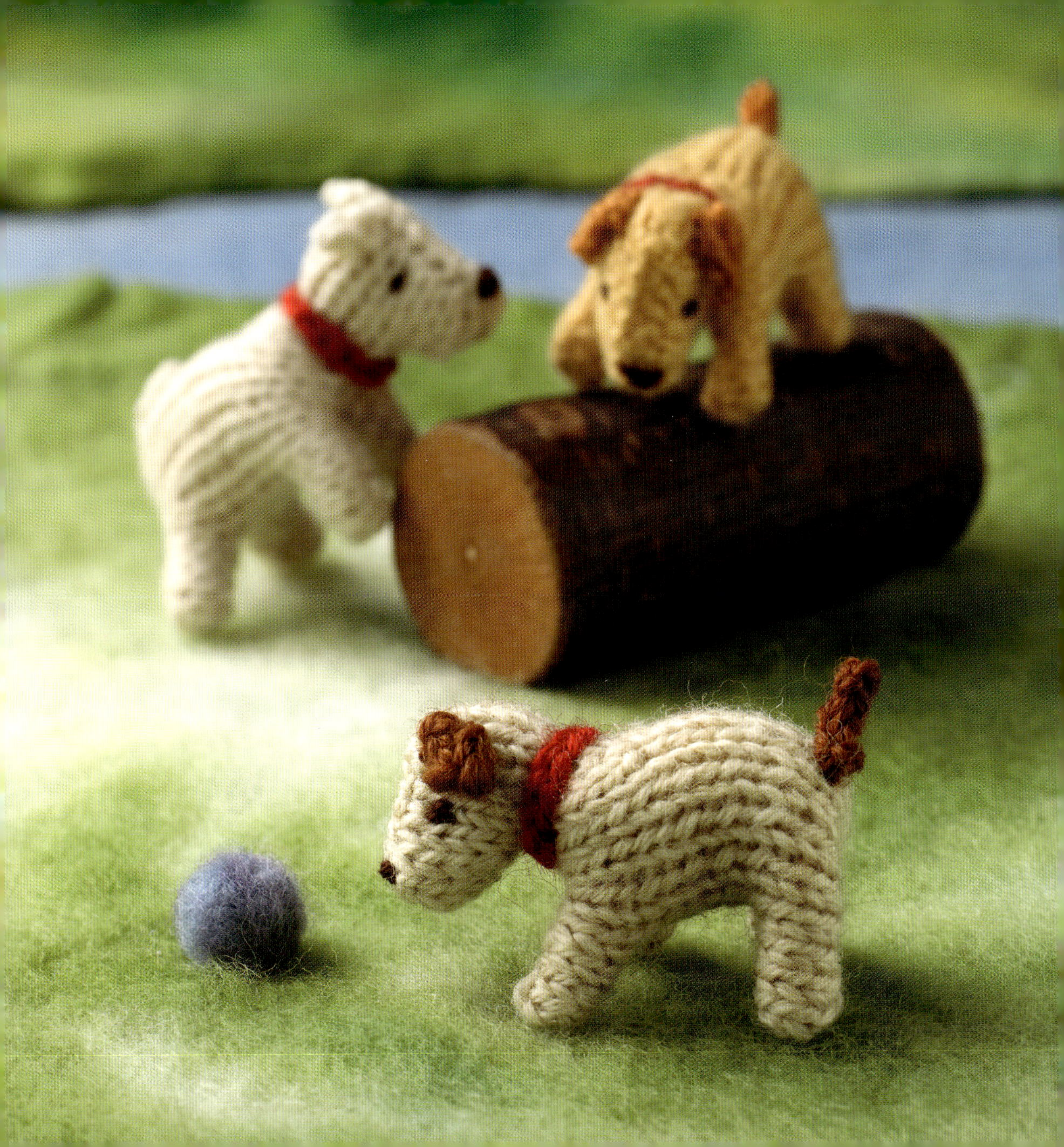

PONY

Materials

- 6g (⅙oz) of DK (light worsted/8-ply) yarn in brown (A) and small amounts in dark brown (B)
- Small amount of 4-ply (fingering) yarn in brown (C)
- Stuffing

Size

8cm (3¼in) long

Difficulty level

Intermediate

Instructions

Body

Using yarn A, cast on 32 sts.
Rows 1–6: beg with a k RS row, work 6 rows in st/st.
Row 7: cast off 7 sts, k to end (25 sts).
Row 8: cast off 7 sts, p to end (18 sts).
Row 9: cast on 3 sts, k to end (21 sts).
Row 10: cast on 3 sts, p to end (24 sts).
Rows 11–16: work 6 rows in st/st.
Row 17: cast off 3 sts, k to end (21 sts).
Row 18: cast off 3 sts, p to end (18 sts).
Row 19: cast on 7 sts, k these 7 sts, k8, (kf/b) twice, k to end (27 sts).
Row 20: cast on 7 sts, p to end (34 sts).
Row 21: k16, (kf/b) twice, k to end (36 sts).
Row 22: p to end.
Row 23: k17, (kf/b) twice, k to end (38 sts).
Row 24: p to end.
Row 25: cast off 7 sts, k10, (kf/b) twice, k to end (33 sts).
Row 26: cast off 7 sts, p to end (26 sts).
Row 27: cast off 7 sts, k to end (19 sts).
Row 28: cast off 7 sts, p to end (12 sts).
Row 29: cast on 3 sts, k to end (15 sts).
Row 30: cast on 3 sts, p to end (18 sts).
Rows 31 and 32: work 2 rows in st/st.
Cast off.

Ears: make two

Using yarn A, cast on 2 sts.
Row 1: p to end.
Row 2: k2tog (1 st).
Fasten off.

Tail

Make a tail (see pages 16–17) using yarn C.

Mane

Make a mane (see page 16) using yarn C.

Making up

Referring to the basic animal assembly on pages 13–17 sew and stuff the legs and body. Sew the ears, tail and mane in place. Using yarn B, work a French knot for each eye.

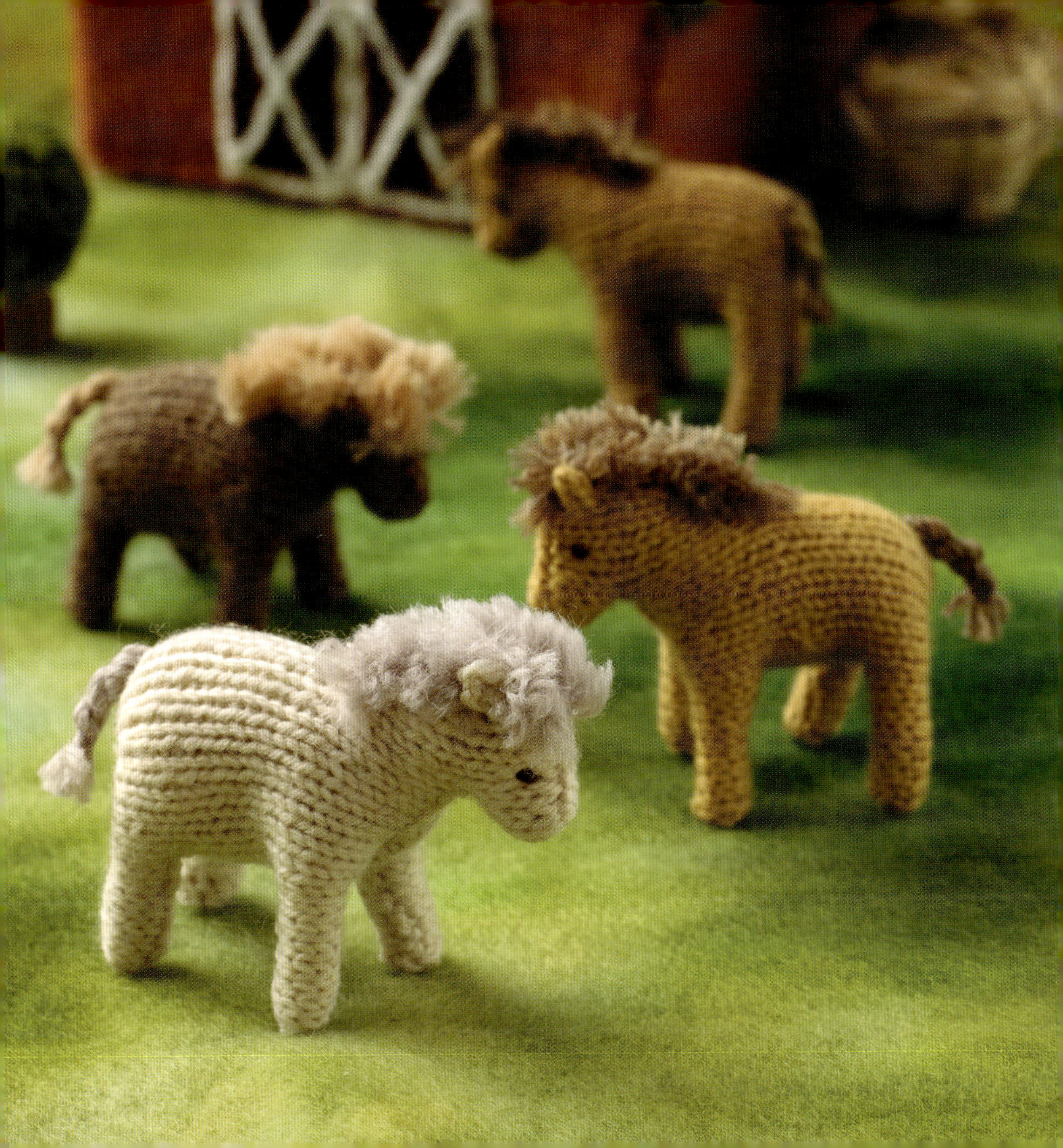

DONKEY

Materials

- 10g (¼oz) of DK (light worsted/8-ply) yarn in grey (A) and small amount in dark brown (B)
- Small amount of 4-ply (fingering) yarn in dark brown (C)
- Piece of card 1.5 x 5cm (½ x 2in)
- Stuffing

Size

8cm (3¼in) long

Difficulty level

Intermediate

Instructions

Body

Using yarn A, cast on 30 sts.
Rows 1–6: beg with a k RS row, work 6 rows in st/st.
Row 7: cast off 6 sts, k to end (24 sts).
Row 8: cast off 6 sts, p to end (18 sts).
Row 9: cast on 3 sts, k to end (21 sts).
Row 10: cast on 3 sts, p to end (24 sts).
Rows 11–16: work 6 rows in st/st.
Row 17: cast off 3 sts, k to end (21 sts).
Row 18: cast off 3 sts, p to end (18 sts).
Row 19: cast on 6 sts, k these 6 sts, k8, (kf/b) twice, k to end (26 sts).
Row 20: cast on 6 sts, p to end (32 sts).
Row 21: k15, (kf/b) twice, k to end (34 sts).
Row 22: p to end.
Row 23: k16, (kf/b) twice, k to end (36 sts).
Row 24: p to end.
Row 25: cast off 6 sts, k to end (30 sts).
Row 26: cast off 6 sts, p to end (24 sts).
Rows 27 and 28: rep rows 25 and 26 once more (12 sts).
Row 29: cast on 4 sts, k to end (16 sts).
Row 30: cast on 4 sts, p to end (20 sts).
Rows 31 and 32: work 2 rows in st/st.
Cast off.

Ears: make two

Using yarn A, cast on 4 sts.
Beg with a p WS row, work in st/st for 5 rows.
Row 6: k2tog twice (2 sts).
Row 7: p2tog (1 st).
Fasten off.

Tail

Make a tail (see pages 16–17) using yarn C.

Mane

Make a mane (see pages 16) using yarn B.

To make up

Referring to the basic animal assembly on pages 13–17, sew and stuff the legs and body. Sew the ears, mane and tail in place on the body. Using yarn B, work a French knot for each eye.

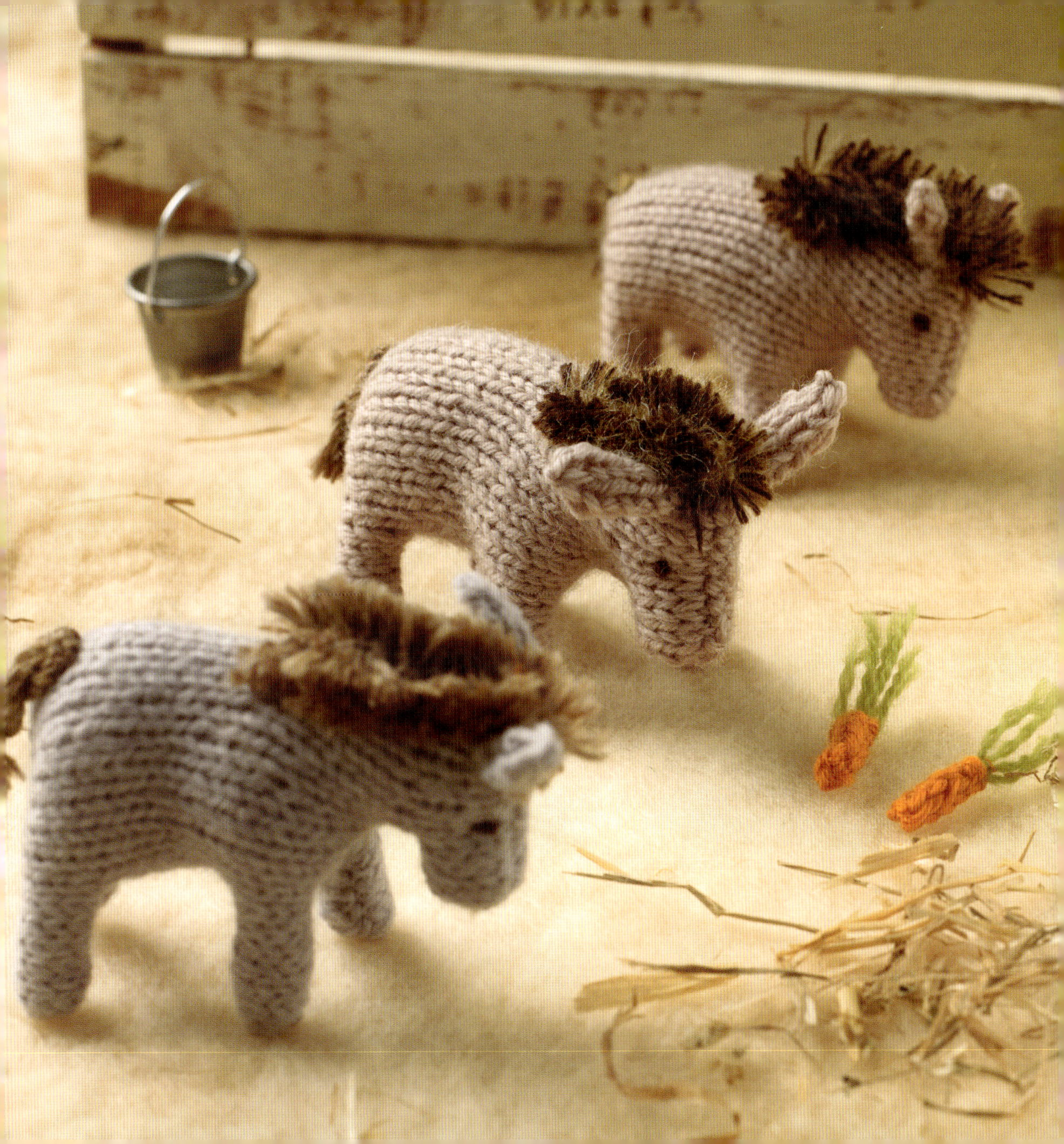

ALPACA

Materials

- 12g (½oz) of fleecy chunky (bulky) yarn in white (A)
- Small amounts of DK (light worsted/8-ply) yarn in cream (B) and 4-ply (fingering) yarn in dark brown (C)
- Stuffing

Additional equipment

2.75mm (UK 12/US 2) and 3.5mm (UK 9 or 10/US 4) knitting needles

Size

8cm (3¼in) tall

Difficulty level

Intermediate

Instructions

Body

Using yarn A and 3.5mm (UK 9, US 4) needles, cast on 20 sts.
Rows 1–6: k to end.
Row 7: cast off 4 sts, k to end (16 sts).
Row 8: as row 7 (12 sts).
Row 9: cast on 2 sts, k to end (14 sts).
Row 10: as row 9 (16 sts).
Rows 11–15: k to end.
Row 16: cast off 2 sts, k to end (14 sts).
Row 17: as row 16 (12 sts).
Row 18: cast on 4 sts, k to end (16 sts).
Row 19: cast on 4 sts, k these 4 sts, k5, (kf/b) twice, k to end (22 sts).
Row 20: k10, (kf/b) twice, k to end (24 sts).
Row 21: k11, (kf/b) twice, k to end (26 sts).
Row 22: k12, (kf/b) twice, k to end (28 sts).
Row 23: k13, (kf/b) twice, k to end (30 sts).
Row 24: k14, (kf/b) twice, k to end (32 sts).
Row 25: cast off 4 sts, k10, (kf/b) twice, k to end (30 sts).
Row 26: as row 25 (28 sts).
Row 27: cast off 7 sts, k to end (21 sts).
Row 28: as row 27 (14 sts).
Rows 29 and 30: k to end.
Row 31: k2tog, (k1, k2tog) to end (9 sts).
Cast off.

Tail

Using yarn A, cast on 5 sts. Work 4 rows in g-st.
Break yarn and thread through all sts, pull tightly and fasten off.

Face

Using yarn B and 2.75mm (UK 12/US 2) needles, cast on 10 sts. Beg with a p WS row, work in st/st for 5 rows.
Break yarn and thread through all sts, pull tightly and fasten off.

Ears: make two

Using yarn B and 2.75mm (UK 12/US 2) needles, cast on 4 sts.
Row 1: (p2tog) twice (2 sts).
Row 2: skpo (1 st).
Fasten off.

To make up

Refer to the basic animal assembly on pages 13–17. Starting between the front legs, sew the underside of the front body/neck closed. Seam the face from the fastened-off end, leaving the cast-on edge open. Insert the face into the head opening and secure it with small stitches around the face edge. Stuff the legs and body and sew the rest of the body closed. Using yarn A, work a running stitch around the neck and pull gently to shape the head. Sew the ears and tail in place. Using yarn C, work a French knot for each eye, then embroider the nose and mouth using backstitch.

Note: if you think the neck is leaning too far forwards, thread a length of yarn A onto a needle. Beginning at the tummy, make a running stitch up the spine towards the head and back down to the tummy. Pull on the yarn gently to shape. Secure the yarn ends and hide them inside the body.

SHEEPDOG

Materials

- Small amounts of DK (light worsted/8-ply) yarn in white (A), black (B) and brown (C)
- Small amount of fleecy chunky (bulky) yarn in white (D)
- Stuffing

Size

6cm (2½in) long

Difficulty level

Intermediate

Instructions

Body

Note: the sheepdog is sitting down and therefore only the front legs are visible. Starting with the right leg and using yarn A, cast on 8 sts.

Rows 1–3: beg with a p WS row, work 3 rows in st/st.
Row 4: k1, k2tog, k2, k2tog, k1 (6 sts).
Rows 5–7: work 3 rows in st/st.
Break yarn, place sts on a holder.

Left leg

Rep rows 1–7 as for right leg but do not break yarn.
Row 8: k across 6 left leg sts then k across 6 held right leg sts (12 sts).
Row 9: p2tog, p to last 2 sts, p2tog (10 sts).
Row 10: k2tog, k to last 2 sts, k2tog (8 sts).
Row 11: as row 9 (6 sts).
Row 12: using yarn A, cast on 3 sts, using yarn A k these 3 sts, using yarn B k6 (9 sts).
Row 13: using yarn A, cast on 3 sts, using yarn A p these 3 sts, changing colours as set, p to end (12 sts).
Row 14: using yarn A, kf/b, k1, using yarn B k8, using yarn A k1, kf/b (14 sts).
Row 15: changing colours as set, p to end.
Row 16: changing colours as set, (kf/b) four times, k to last 4 sts, (kf/b) four times (22 sts).
Row 17: using yarn A p5, using yarn B, p to last 5 sts, using yarn A p5.
Row 18: changing colours as set, k4, (kf/b) three times, k8, (kf/b) three times, k4 (28 sts).
Row 19: p to end.
Row 20: k to end.
Row 21: (p2, p2tog) to end (21 sts).
Row 22: (k2tog, k1) to end (14 sts).
Break yarn, thread through all sts and pull tightly. Fasten off.

Head

Using yarn B, cast on 7 sts.
Row 1: p to end.
Row 2: (kf/b) to end (14 sts).
Row 3: pf/b, p to end (15 sts).
Row 4: using yarn B k7, using yarn A k1, using yarn B k7.
Rows 5–7: changing colours as set, work 3 rows in st/st.
Row 8: changing colours as set, k3, k2tog, k5, k2tog, k3 (13 sts).
Row 9: break yarn B and p to end using yarn A only.
Row 10: (k2, k2tog) to last st, k1 (10 sts).
Row 11: p to end.
Break yarn, thread through all sts and pull tightly. Fasten off.

Ears: make two

Using yarn B, cast on 4 sts.
Row 1: k to end.
Row 2: p2tog twice (2 sts).
Row 3: k2tog (1 st).
Fasten off.

Tail

Using yarn B, cast on 5 sts.
Row 1: p to end.
Row 2: k2tog, k1, k2tog (3 sts).
Break yarn, thread through all sts and pull tightly. Fasten off.

Making up

Sew each leg from the paw up. Sew the body almost completely closed, leaving an opening for stuffing. Stuff the legs and body and secure the legs to the body with a couple of small stitches. Sew the head seam, stuff and work running stitch along the cast-on edge, pulling tightly to close. Sew the head to the body. Sew the ears and tail in place. Using yarn C, work a French knot for each eye. Using yarn B, work a large French knot for the nose. Cut a length of yarn D and wrap around the neck twice. Hide the yarn ends inside the body.

SHEEP

Materials

- Small amount of fleecy chunky (bulky) yarn in white (A)
- Small amount of DK (light worsted/8-ply) yarn in white or black (for head, ears and tail) (B)
- Small amount of 4-ply (fingering) yarn in brown (C)
- Stuffing

Additional equipment

- Body: 3mm (UK 11, US 2/3) knitting needles
- Head, ears and tail: 2.75mm (UK 12, US 2) knitting needles

Size

6cm (2½in) long

Difficulty level

Beginner

Body

Using yarn A and 3mm (UK 11, US 2/3) needles, cast on 14 sts. Work 20 rows in g-st.
Break yarn, thread through all sts and pull tightly. Fasten off.

Head

Using yarn B and 2.75mm (UK 12, US 2) needles, cast on 13 sts.
Work 8 rows in st/st.
Break yarn, thread through all sts and pull tightly. Fasten off.

Ears: make two

Using yarn B and 2.75mm (UK 12, US 2) needles, cast on 3 sts.
Row 1: p2tog, p1 (2 sts).
Row 2: skpo (1 st).
Fasten off.

Tail

Using yarn B and 2.75mm (UK 12, US 2) needles, cast on 3 sts. Work an i-cord for 3 rows. Break yarn, thread through all sts and pull tightly. Fasten off.

To make up

Sew the body seam and stuff. Work running stitch along the cast-on edge and pull tight. Finish the head in the same way. Sew the head to the body, then sew the ears and tail in place. Using yarn C (or white yarn for black-faced sheep), work a French knot for each eye. Using yarn C, embroider the nose with backstitches.

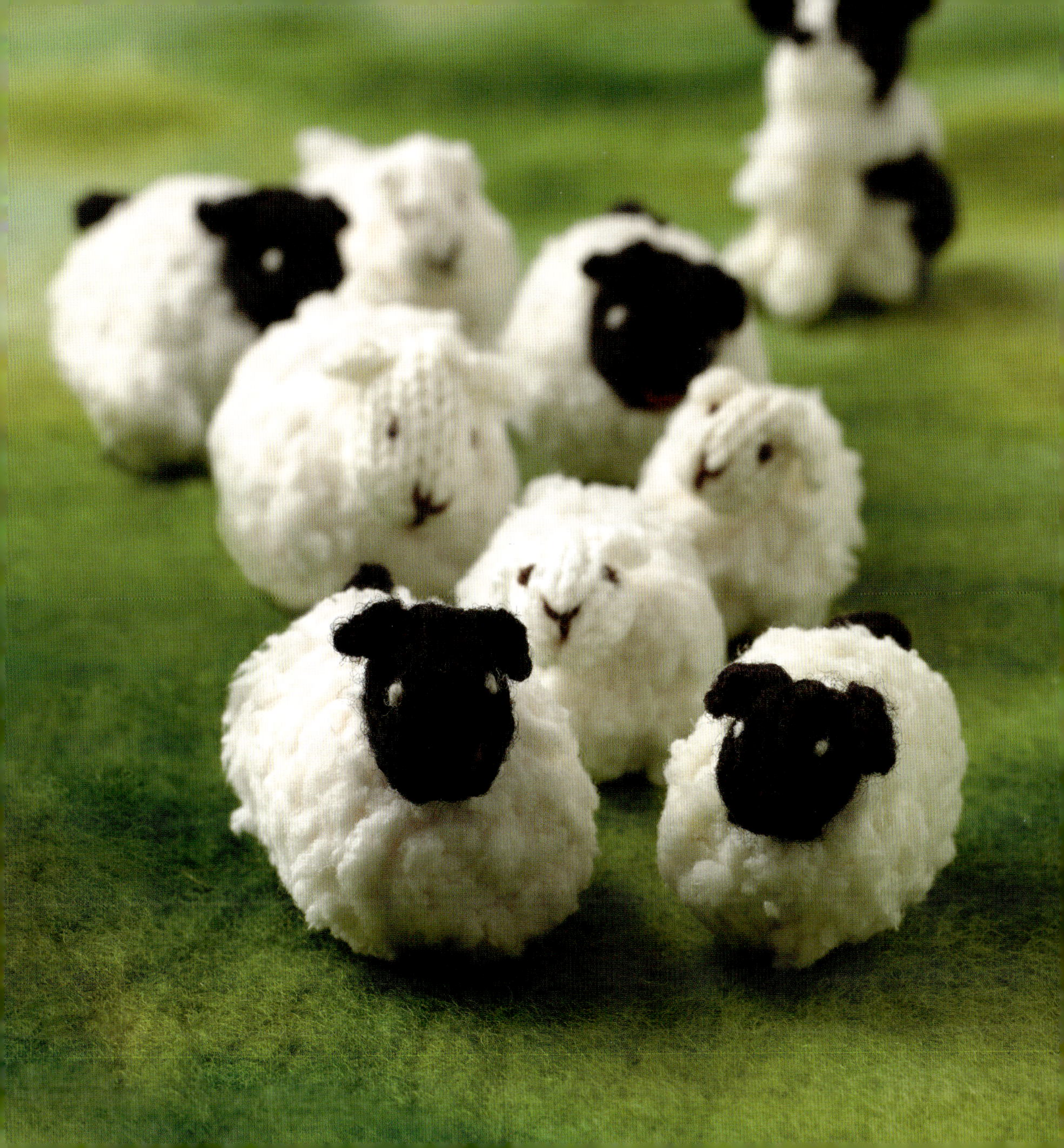

PIG & PIGLETS

Materials

For the pig:
- 5g (⅙oz) of DK (light worsted/8-ply) yarn in pale pink (A)
- Small amount of 4-ply (fingering) yarn in brown (B)
- Stuffing

For the piglet:
- Small amount of DK (light worsted/8-ply) yarn in pale pink (A)
- Small amount of 4-ply (fingering) yarn in brown (B)
- Stuffing

Size

Pig: 5cm (2in) long; piglet: 4cm (1½in) long

Difficulty level

Intermediate

Instructions

Pig

Body
Using yarn A, cast on 20 sts.
Rows 1–5: beg with a k RS row, work 5 rows in st/st.
Row 6: cast off 2 sts, p to end (18 sts).
Row 7: cast off 2 sts, k to end (16 sts).
Row 8: cast on 2 sts, p to end (18 sts).
Row 9: cast on 2 sts, k to end (20 sts).
Rows 10–13: work 4 rows in st/st.
Rows 14–17: as rows 6–9 (20 sts).
Rows 18 and 19: work 2 rows in st/st.
Row 20: cast off 2 sts, p to end (18 sts).
Row 21: cast off 2 sts, k6, k2tog, k to end (15 sts).
Row 22: cast off 2 sts, p to end (13 sts).
Row 23: cast off 2 sts, k to end (11 sts).
Row 24: p to end.
Row 25: k4, k2tog, k to end (10 sts).
Row 26: p to end.
Row 27: k4, k2tog, k4 (9 sts).
Row 28: p to end.
Row 29 (g-st ridge for snout): p to end.
Row 30: p to end.
Break yarn, thread through all sts and pull tightly. Fasten off.

Ears: make two
Using yarn A, cast on 4 sts.
Row 1: (p2tog) twice (2 sts).
Row 2: skpo (1 st).
Fasten off.

Tail
Using yarn A, cast on 2 sts. Work in i-cord for 3 rows. Pass the first st over the second and fasten off.

To make up
Referring to the basic animal assembly on pages 13–17, sew up the body, head and legs and stuff. Sew the ears and tail in place. Using yarn B, work a French knot for each eye and embroider nostrils with short backstitches.

Piglet

Body

Using yarn A, cast on 14 sts.
Rows 1–4: beg with a k RS row, work 5 rows in st/st.
Row 5: cast off 2 sts, k to end (12 sts).
Row 6: cast off 2 sts, p to end (10 sts).
Row 7: cast on 2 sts, k to end (12 sts).
Row 8: cast on 2 sts, p to end (14 sts).
Rows 9 and 10: work 2 rows in st/st.
Rows 11–16: as rows 5–10 (14 sts).
Row 17: cast off 3 sts, k to end (11 sts).
Row 18: cast off 3 sts, p to end (8 sts).
Row 19: k3, k2tog, k to end (7 sts).
Rows 20–24: work 5 rows in st/st.
Row 25 (g-st ridge for snout):
p to end.
Row 26: p to end.
Break yarn, thread through all sts and pull tightly. Fasten off.

Ears: make two

Work as given for the adult pig but split the strand of yarn A in half before beginning. Alternatively, work a backstitch in the same spot three times for each ear.

Tail

Using yarn A, cast on 2 sts. Work in i-cord for 2 rows. Pass the first st over the second and fasten off.

To make up

Make up as for the pig.

HEN AND CHICKS

Materials

For the hen:
- Small amounts of DK (light worsted/8-ply) yarn in white (A) and red (C)
- Small amounts of 4-ply (fingering) yarn in yellow (B) and dark brown (D)
- For the cockerel variation: Small amounts of DK (light worsted/8-ply) yarn in brown (A), red brown (E), and red (C)
- Small amounts of 4-ply (fingering) yarn in yellow (B) and dark brown (D)

For the chick:
- Small amounts of 4-ply (fingering) yarn in soft yellow (A), yellow (B) and dark brown (C)
- Stuffing

Size

Hen and cockerel: 3.5cm (1½in) long; chick: 2.5cm (1in) long

Difficulty level

Beginner

Instructions

Hen

Body

Using yarn A, cast on 12 sts.
Work 20 rows in g-st.
Cast off.

Beak

Using yarn B, cast on 2 sts.
Next row: p2tog (1 st). Fasten off.

To make up

Fold the body piece diagonally to make a triangle, stuff and sew the seam closed. Thread a needle with a length of yarn A and make small ladder stitches to the top centre of the body, then take the needle out from the base of the body. Pull on the thread to shape the back and hide the yarn end inside the body. Sew the beak in place. Using yarn C, add the comb and wattle by making backstitches, leaving small loops: make three loops for the comb, and two for the wattle. Using yarn A, work backstitches at the tail end, leaving a loose loop every other stitch until there are three or four loops. Cut each loop open for a feathery tail.
Using yarn D, work a French knot for each eye.

Variation: cockerel

Body

Using yarn A, cast on 12 sts.
Work 10 rows in g-st.
Row 11: using yarn E k6, using yarn A k6.
Rows 12–20: rep row 11, twisting the yarns together at each colour change to prevent gaps.
Cast off.

Beak

Work as given for hen.

To make up

Make up as given for hen.

Chick

Body

Using yarn A, cast on 8 sts.
Work 10 rows in g-st.
Cast off.

Beak

Work as for hen.

To make up

Make up as for hen, omitting comb, wattle and tail, and using yarn D to embroider chick's eyes.

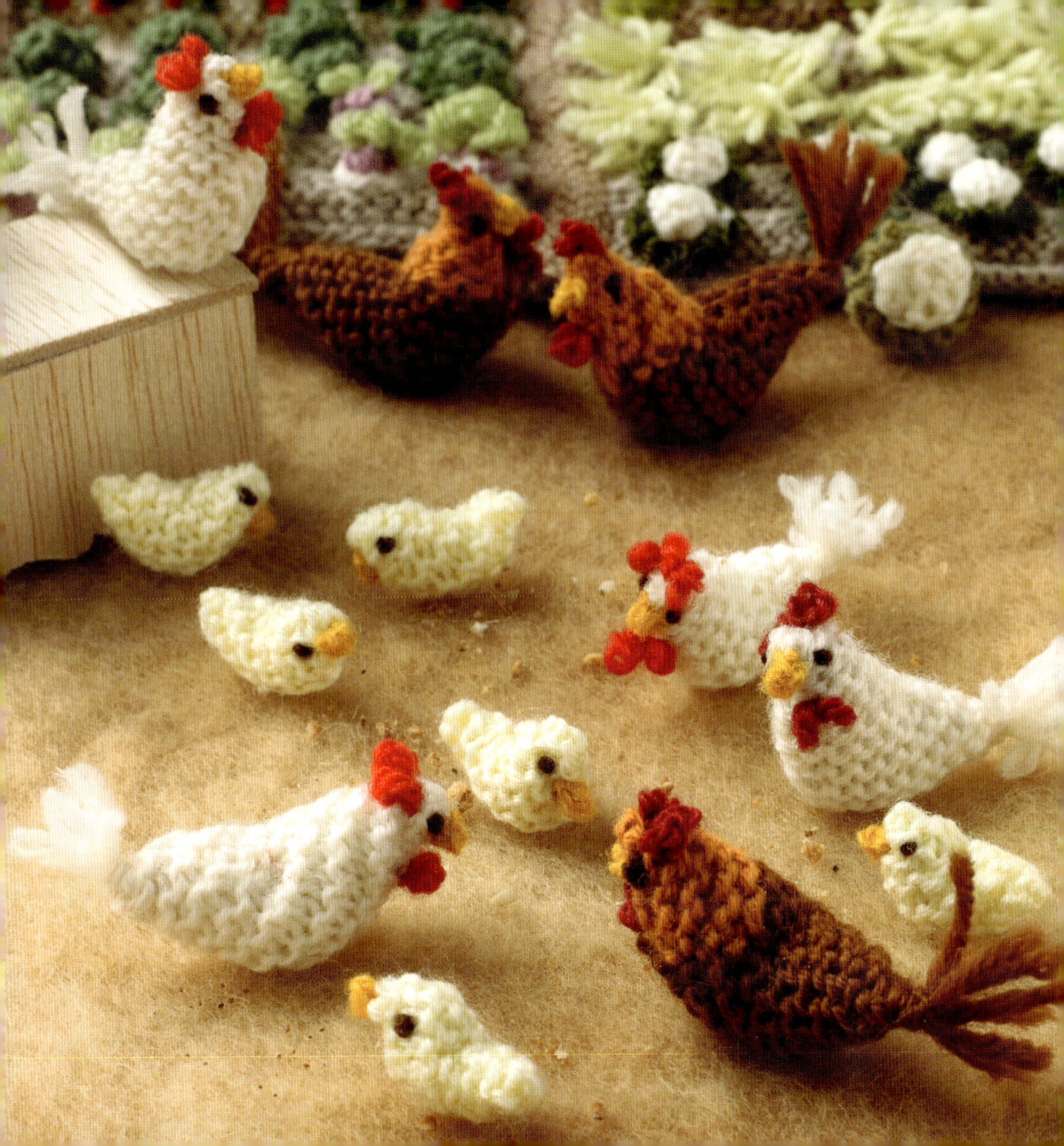

GOAT

Materials

For white goat:
- 7g (⅕ oz) of DK (light worsted/8-ply) yarn in white (A) and small amount in dark brown (B)

For black goat:
- 7g (⅕ oz) of DK (light worsted/8-ply) yarn in black (A) and small amounts in light brown (B) and white (C)
- Stuffing

Size
7cm (2¾in) long

Difficulty level
Intermediate

Instructions

Body
Using yarn A, cast on 22 sts.
Rows 1–5: beg with a k RS row, work 5 rows in st/st.
Row 6: cast off 4 sts, p to end (18 sts).
Row 7: cast off 4 sts, k to end (14 sts).
Row 8: cast on 2 sts, p to end (16 sts).
Row 9: cast on 2 sts, k to end (18 sts).
Rows 10–15: work 6 rows in st/st.
Row 16: cast off 2 sts, p to end (16 sts).
Row 17: cast off 2 sts, k to end (14 sts).
Row 18: cast on 4 sts, p to end (18 sts).
Row 19: cast on 4 sts, k these 4 sts, k6, (kf/b) twice, k to end (24 sts).
Row 20: p to end.
Row 21: k11, (kf/b) twice, k to end (26 sts).
Row 22: p to end.
Row 23: k12, (kf/b) twice, k to end (28 sts).
Row 24: cast off 4 sts, p to end (24 sts).
Row 25: cast off 4 sts, k to end (20 sts).
Row 26: Cast off 5 sts, p to end (15 sts).
Row 27: cast off 5 sts, k to end (10 sts).
Row 28: cast on 3 sts, p to end (13 sts).
Row 29: cast on 3 sts, k to end (16 sts).
Rows 30 and 31: work 2 rows in st/st.
Row 32: p2tog, cast off the st on the right needle, cast off all sts to the last 2 sts, p2tog, cast off last remaining st.

Ears: make two
Using yarn A, cast on 2 sts.
Row 1: p to end.
Row 2: k2tog (1 st).
Fasten off.

Horns: make two
Using yarn B, cast on 2 sts. Work an i-cord for 4 rows, pass the first st over the second and fasten off.

Tail
Using yarn A, work as given for the horns.

To make up
Referring to the basic animal assembly on pages 13–17, sew and stuff the legs and body. Thread a needle with a length of yarn A (for white goat) or yarn C (for black goat) and make 6–8 backstitches over the chin, leaving a loop every other stitch. Cut the loops open and separate the strands. Sew the ears, horns and tail in place. Using yarn B (for white goat) or yarn C (for black goat), work a French knot for each eye.

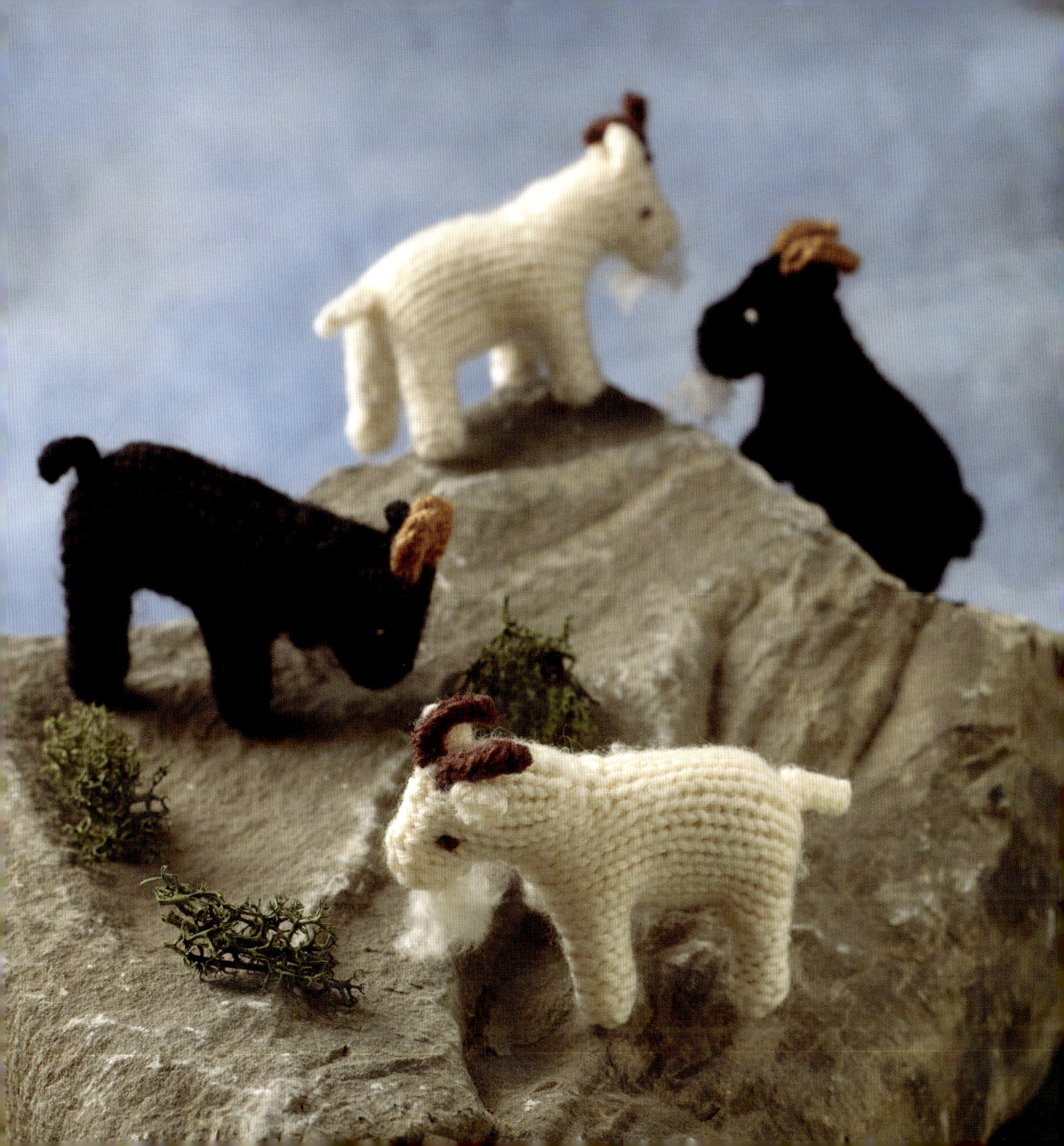

TURKEY

Materials

- Small amounts of DK (light worsted/8-ply) yarn in light blue (B), sandy brown (C), black (D), dark brown (E) and pink (F)
- Small amounts of DK (light worsted/8-ply) yarn in white and black mix or create mix yarn by holding two strands of 4-ply (fingering) yarn in black and white together (A)
- Stuffing

Size

6cm (2½in) long (excluding tail feathers)

Difficulty level

Intermediate

Instructions

Body

Using yarn A, cast on 12 sts.
Rows 1–4: beg with a k RS row, work 4 rows in st/st.
Row 5: (k1, kf/b) to end (18 sts).
Rows 6–10: work 5 rows in st/st.
Row 11: k13, yf, sl1, yb, turn work.
Row 12: sl1, p8, yb, sl1, yf, turn work.
Row 13: sl1, k8, yf, sl1, yb, turn work.
Row 14: sl1, p7, yb, sl1, yf, turn work.
Row 15: sl1, k to end.
Rows 16–22: work 7 rows in st/st.
Row 23: k2tog to end (9 sts).
Row 24: change to yarn B, p to end.
Row 25: k2, k2tog, k1, k2tog, k2 (7 sts).
Rows 26–29: work 4 rows in st/st.
Row 30: p2, pf/b, p1, pf/b, p2 (9 sts).
Rows 31 and 32: work 2 rows in st/st.
Row 33: k2tog to last st, k1 (5 sts).
Break yarn, thread through all sts and pull tightly. Fasten off.

Tail

Using yarn C, cast on 26 sts.
Row 1: k2, (p2, k2) to end.
Row 2: change to yarn D, p2, (k2, p2) to end.
Row 3: change to yarn E, k2, (p2, k2) to end.
Row 4: p2 (k2, p2) to end.
Row 5: k2, (p2, k2) to end.
Row 6: p2, (k2, p2) to end.
Row 7: change to yarn C, k2, (p2tog, k2) to end (20 sts).
Row 8: change to yarn E, p2, (k1, p2) to end.
Row 9: k2tog, (p1, k2tog) to end (13 sts).
Row 10: p1, (k1, p1) to end.
Break yarn, thread through all sts and pull tightly. Fasten off.

Wings: make two

Using yarn D, cast on 12 sts.
Rows 1–3: beg with a p WS row, work 3 rows in st/st.
Rows 4: (using yarn C k1, using yarn E k1) to end.
Rows 5 and 6: changing colours as set, work 2 rows in st/st.
Row 7: fasten off yarn E and continue with yarn C only, (k2, k2tog) to end (9 sts).
Break yarn, thread through all sts and pull tightly. Fasten off.

Wattle

Using yarn F, cast on 3 sts.
Row 1: p to end.
Row 2: k1, skpo (2 sts).
Row 3: p to end.
Row 4: skpo (1 st).
Fasten off.

Beak

Using yarn F, cast on 3 sts. Work an i-cord for 1 row. Continuing to work the i-cord:
Row 2: k1, skpo (2 sts).
Row 3: k to end.
Row 4: skpo (1 st).
Fasten off.

To make up

Stuff the body and close the body seam (this will be at the top of the body). Sew the tail in place. Seam and attach the wings. Attach the beak and wattle to the face. Using yarn E, work a French knot for each eye.

PHEASANT

Materials

For the cock pheasant:
- Small amounts of DK (light worsted/8-ply) yarn in brown (A), white (B), green (C) and red (D)
- Small amounts of 4-ply (fingering) yarn in yellow (E) and dark brown (F)

For the hen pheasant:
- Small amounts of DK (light worsted/8-ply) yarn in light brown mix (A) and dark brown mix (B)
- Small amounts of 4-ply (fingering) yarn in yellow (C) and dark brown (D)
- Stuffing

Size

5cm (2in)

Difficulty level

Beginner

Instructions

Cock pheasant

Body
Using yarn A, cast on 7 sts.
Row 1: p to end.
Row 2: k2, kf/b, k1, kf/b, k2 (9 sts).
Row 3: p to end.
Row 4: k1, (kf/b, k1) to end (13 sts).
Row 5: p to end.
Row 6: (k2, kf/b) to last st, k1 (17 sts).
Rows 7–10: work 4 rows in st/st.
Row 11 (short row): p12, yb, sl1, yf, turn work.
Row 12 (short row): sl1, k7, yf, sl1, yb, turn work.
Row 13 (short row): sl1, p6, yb, sl1, yf, turn work.
Row 14: sl1, k to end.
Row 15: p to end.
Row 16: k1, (k2tog) to end (9 sts).
Row 17: p to end.
Row 18: change to yarn B, k to end.
Rows 19 and 20: change to yarn C and work 2 rows in st/st.
Rows 21–23: change to yarn D and work 3 rows in st/st.
Break yarn, thread through all sts and pull tightly. Fasten off.

Wings: make two
Using yarn A, cast on 8 sts.
Rows 1–4: beg with a p WS row, work 4 rows in st/st.
Row 5: p1, p2tog, p2, p2tog, p1 (6 sts).
Row 6: k to end.
Row 7: p2tog to end (3 sts).
Break yarn, thread through all sts and pull tightly. Fasten off.

Tail
Using yarn A, cast on 3 sts.
Rows 1–8: work 8 rows in g-st.
Row 9: skpo, k1 (2 sts).
Rows 10–12: work 3 rows in g-st.
Row 13: k2tog (1 st).
Fasten off.

Beak
Using yarn E, cast on 2 sts.
Row 1: k to end, pass first st over the second and fasten off.
Alternatively, you can embroider the beak on the head by working backstitches in the same spot a few times.

To make up
Stuff the body and close the body seam (this will be at the top of the body). Seam the wings and sew to each side of the body. Sew the beak and tail in place. Using yarn F work a French knot for each eye.

Hen pheasant

Body
Work as given for cock pheasant, using yarn A.

Wings: make two
Work as given for cock pheasant, using yarn B.

Tail
Using yarn A, cast on 3 sts.
Rows 1–4: work 4 rows in g-st.
Row 5: skpo, k1 (2 sts).
Rows 6–8: work 3 rows in g-st.
Row 9: k2tog (1 st). Fasten off.

Beak
Work as given for cock pheasant, using yarn C.

To make up
Make up as for cock pheasant, using yarn D to work a French knot for each eye.

MAGPIE & CROW

Materials

For the magpie:
- Small amounts of DK (light worsted/8-ply) yarn in white (A), black (B) and blue (C)
- Small amounts of 4-ply (fingering) yarn in black (D) (alternatively, split a length of yarn B in half for yarn D)

For the crow:
- Small amounts of DK (light worsted/8-ply) yarn in black (A)
- Small amounts of 4-ply (fingering) yarn in black (B) (alternatively, split a length of yarn A in half for yarn B), white (C), and light brown (D)
- Stuffing

Size

3cm (1¼in) tall

Difficulty level

Beginner

Instructions

Magpie

Body

Using yarn A, cast on 5 sts.
Row 1: (kf/b) to end (10 sts).
Row 2: p to end.
Row 3: (k1, kf/b) to end (15 sts).
Row 4 (g-st ridge): k to end.
Row 5: k to end.
Row 6: p to end.
Row 7: k2tog, k to last 2 sts, k2tog (13 sts).
Row 8: change to yarn B and p to end.
Row 9: (k1, k2tog) to last st, k1 (9 sts).
Rows 10–14: work 5 rows in st/st.
Row 15: (k1, k2tog) to end (6 sts).
Break yarn, thread through all sts and pull tightly. Fasten off.

Wings: make two

Using yarn A, cast on 6 sts.
Row 1: p to end.
Rows 2 and 3: change to yarn C and work 2 rows in st/st.
Row 4: (k1, k2tog) twice (4 sts).
Row 5: p to end.
Row 6: (k2tog) twice (2 sts).
Pass the first st over the second and fasten off.

Beak

Using yarn D, cast on 3 sts.
Row 1: p to end.
Row 2: sl1, k2tog, pass the first st over the second st, fasten off.

Tail

Using yarn C, cast on 3 sts.
Rows 1–5: work 5 rows in g-st.
Row 6: k1, k2tog (2 sts).
Rows 7–8: work 2 rows in g-st.
Pass the first st over the second and fasten off.

To make up

Sew the side seam of the body and stuff. With the cast-on yarn end, work running stitch along the cast-on edge of the body and pull tightly. Sew the rest of the base and close the body. Thread a needle with a length of yarn A and pierce the body from the centre of the base, taking the needle out at the back of neck, then repeat with the other end. Pull gently to flatten the base and secure the yarn ends. Sew the beak and tail in place. Seam the wings and sew to each side of the body. Using yarn A, work a French knot for each eye. Using yarn D, embroider feet with backstitches.

Crow

Body, wings and beak
Work as given for magpie, using yarn A for body and wings, and yarn B for beak.

Tail
Using yarn A, cast on 3 sts.
Rows 1–3: work 3 rows in g-st.
Row 4: skpo, k1 (2 sts).
Row 5: k to end.
Pass the first st over the second and fasten off.

To make up
Make up as given for magpie, using yarn C to work a French knot for each eye and yarn D to embroider the feet.

SCARECROW

Materials

- Small amounts of DK (light worsted/8-ply) yarn in off-white (A), light brown (B), yellow (D) and brown (E)
- Small amounts of 4-ply (fingering) in red brown (C), green (F), pink (G) and dark brown (H)
- Stuffing
- Wooden skewer
- Two circles of cardboard: 1 x 2.5cm (1in), 1 x 3cm (1¼in) in diameter

Additional equipment

Sewing needle

Size

12.5cm (5in) tall

Difficulty level

Intermediate

Instructions

Body

Using yarn A, cast on 7 sts.
Row 1 (WS): p to end.
Row 2: (kf/b) to end (14 sts).
Row 3: p to end.
Row 4: (k1, kf/b) to end (21 sts).
Row 5 (g-st ridge): k to end.
Rows 6 and 7: beg with a k RS row, work 2 rows in st/st.
Row 8: (k4, k2tog) three times, k3 (18 sts).
Rows 9–13: work 5 rows in st/st.
Row 14 (shape neck): (k1, k2tog) to end (12 sts).
Row 15: change to yarn B and p to end.
Row 16: k3, (kf/b) six times, k to end (18 sts).
Rows 17–19: work 3 rows in st/st.
Row 20 (shape eyeline): k3, (k2tog, k1) four times, k3 (14 sts).
Rows 21–23: work 3 rows in st/st.
Row 24: k2, (k2tog, k2) to end (11 sts).
Break yarn, thread through all sts and pull tightly. Fasten off.

Jacket

Using yarn C, cast on 22 sts.
Rows 1–20: beg with a k RS row, work 20 rows in st/st.
Row 21: k1, (k2tog, k1) to end (15 sts).
Cast off.

Sleeves: make two

Using yarn C, cast on 9 sts.
Beg with a p WS row, work 9 rows in st/st.
Next row: k2tog to last st, k1 (5 sts).
Break yarn, thread through all sts and pull tightly. Fasten off.

Gloves

Using yarn D, cast on 6 sts. Beg with a p WS row, work 2 rows in st/st.
Break yarn, thread through all sts and pull tightly. Fasten off.

Hat

Using yarn E, cast on 9 sts.
Row 1: (kf/b) to end (18sts).
Row 2 (g-st ridge): k to end.
Rows 3–6: beg with a k RS row, work 4 rows in st/st.
Row 7 (g-st ridge): p to end.
Row 8: (pf/b) to end (36 sts).
Cast off.

Scarf

Using yarn F, cast on 5 sts.
Work in g-st until piece measures 7cm (2¾in).
Cast off.
To make scarf fringe, cut a 4cm (1¾in) piece of yarn and fold in half. Thread both ends through a needle eye. Insert the needle through the scarf edge and pull partway through, leaving the loop on one side. Remove needle and pass yarn ends through the loop. Pull gently on the yarn ends to tighten the loop and anchor the fringe in place. Repeat several times along each end of scarf. Trim the ends evenly.

Base plate

Using yarn E, cast on 9 sts.
Row 1 (WS): p to end.
Row 2: (kf/b) to end (18 sts).
Row 3: p to end.
Row 4: (k1, kf/b) to end (27 sts).
Row 5: p to end.
Row 6 (g-st ridge): p to end.
Rows 7 and 8: beg with a p WS row, work 2 rows in st/st.
Row 9 (g-st ridge): k to end.
Row 10: k to end.
Row 11: (p1, p2tog) to end (18 sts).
Row 12: k to end.
Row 13: p2tog to end (9 sts).
Break yarn, thread through all sts and pull tightly. Fasten off.

To make up

Using the fastened-off yarn end, sew the head seam down to the neck, then beginning at the bottom, sew the body seam halfway up. With the cast-on yarn end, work running stitch along the cast-on edge and pull tightly. Sew the rest of the base seam, stuff body and close seam. Using yarn A, work running stitch around the neck and pull tightly to shape. Push the needle through the back of the neck up to the eyeline. Make a few running stitches across the front of the face to create indents for the eyes. Oull the yarn tight to form the eyeline, hide the yarn end inside the head and cut the yarn.

Seam the glove and sleeve, then insert the glove into the cuff end and sew it to the sleeve with a few stitches.

Using yarn D, backstitch in the same spot two or three times on each glove to create thumbs. Attach the coat to the body and fold the top edge over at the front to make collars. Stitch the collars down to the body. Using yarn B, make hair by working backstitches on the head, leaving a loop every other stitch. Cut the loops open. Using yarn G, work a French knot for the nose. Using yarn H, work a French knot for each eye. Attach the hat and scarf.

Place the cardboard discs inside the base plate (placing the larger disc on the bottom) and sew partly closed. Stuff and close the seam. Insert the skewer through the base plate and the body.

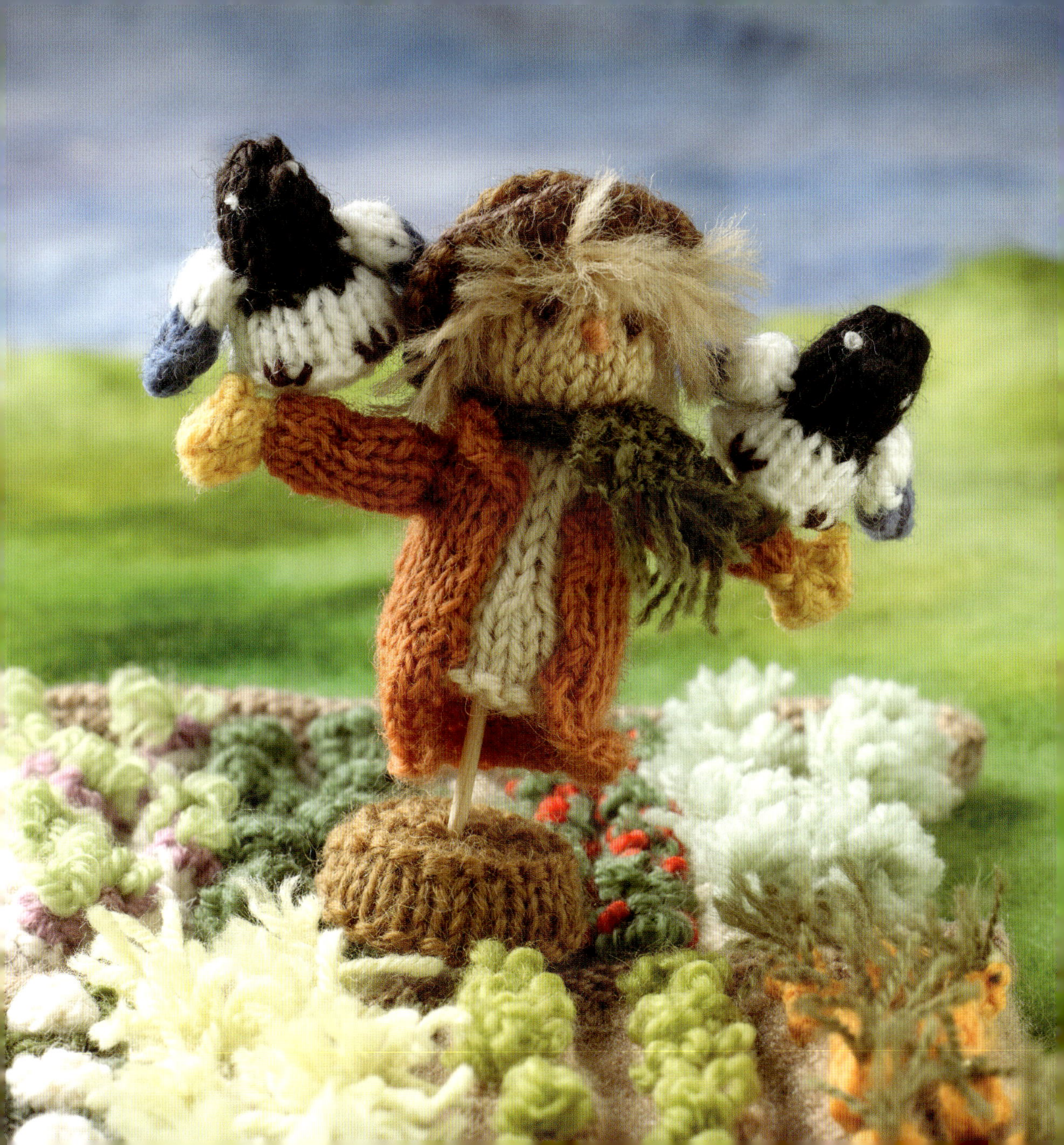

PUMPKIN

Materials
To make one pumpkin:
- Small amount of DK (light worsted/8-ply) yarn in orange (A) and a small amount in green (B)
- Stuffing

Additional equipment
- Optional: 3mm (UK 11, US C/2 or D/3) crochet hook
- Two 2.75mm (UK 2, US 12) double-pointed needles

Size
4cm (1½in) across

Difficulty level
Beginner

Instructions

Body
Using yarn A, cast on 7 sts.
Row 1: p to end.
Row 2: (kf/b) to end (14 sts).
Row 3: p to end.
Row 4: (k1, kf/b) to end (21 sts).
Row 5: p to end.
Row 6: (k2, kf/b) to end (28 sts).
Row 7: p to end.
Row 8: (k3, kf/b) to end (35 sts).
Row 9: (p4, k1) to end.
Row 10: k to end.
Rows 11–16: rep rows 9 and 10 three times.
Row 17: as row 9.
Row 18: (k1, k2tog twice) to end (21 sts).
Row 19: (p2, k1) to end.
Row 20: (k1, k2tog) to end (14 sts).
Break yarn, thread through all sts and pull tightly. Fasten off.

Stalk
Using yarn B and double-pointed needles, cast on 8 sts, leaving a long tail of about 10cm (4in).
Row 1: p to end.
Row 2: (k1, k2tog) twice, k2tog, do not turn (5 sts).
Row 3: with yarn held to back of work, slide the sts to the right-hand side of the needle and k1, k2tog twice, do not turn (3 sts).
Rows 4 and 5: with yarn held to back of work, slide the sts to the right-hand side of the needle, k to end.
Break yarn, leaving a 10cm (4in) tail, thread through all sts and pull tightly. Fasten off.

To make up
Sew the side seam of the pumpkin and stuff. Using the cast-on yarn end, work running stitch along the cast-on end and pull tight. Close the seam. Work a running stitch along each of the ribbed lines and pull tightly to shape. Seam the stalk and attach it to the pumpkin. Optional: using a crochet hook, rejoin yarn B to base of stalk and make 8 chains. Fasten off and hide the yarn end inside the stalk.

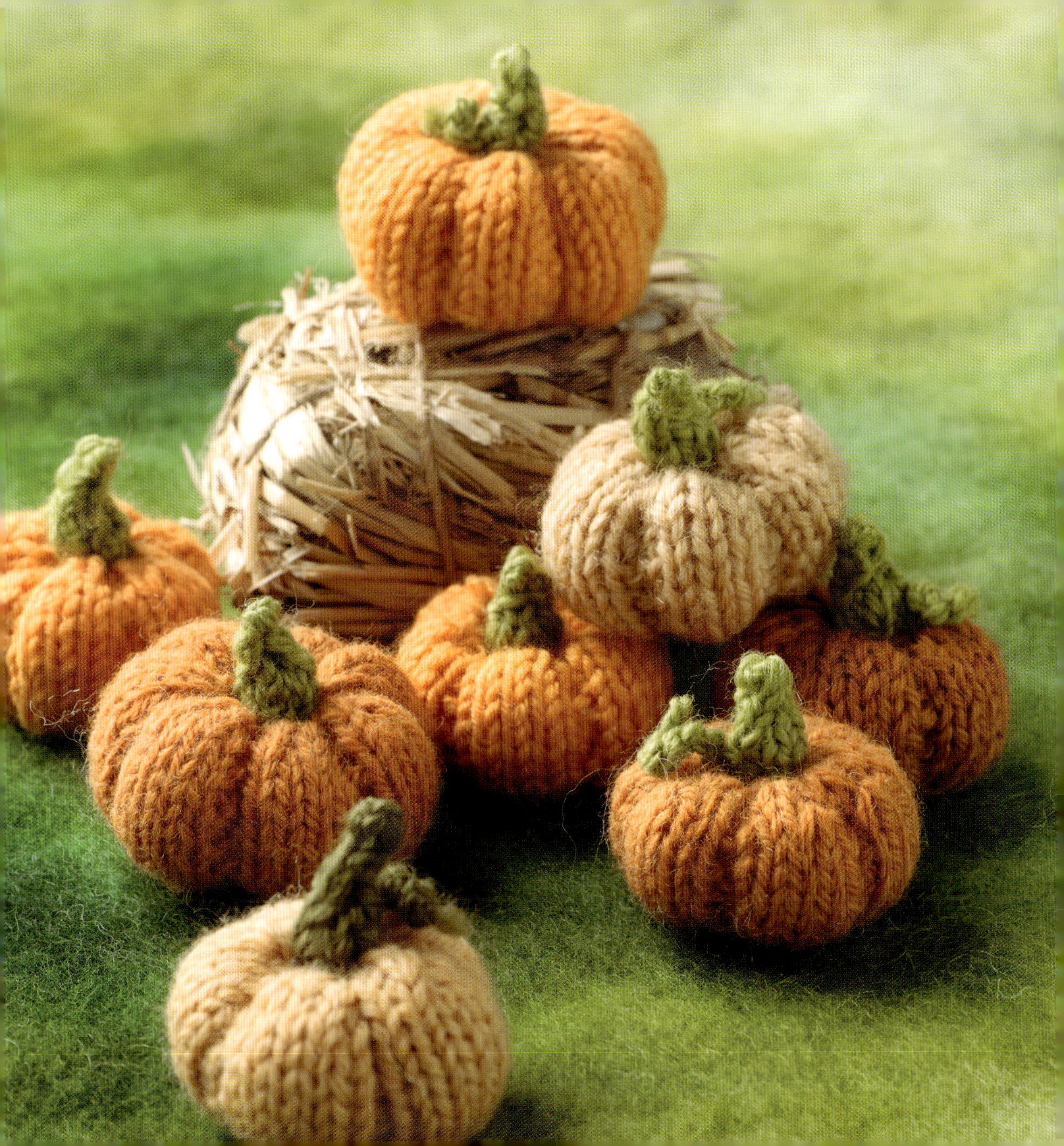

VEGETABLES

Materials

- Small amounts of DK (8-ply) yarn in white (A), light green (B), red (C), orange (E), purple (F) and green (I)
- Small amounts of 4-ply (fingering) yarn in green (D), light purple (G), light green (H), white (J), brown (K), light brown (L), yellow (M) and yellow-green (N)

Sizes

Cauliflower, aubergine/ eggplant and lettuce: 2cm (¾in) across; tomato, orange, apple and potato: 1cm (½in) across; leek: 3cm (1¼in) long; corn: 3cm (1¼in) long; potato sack: 4cm (1½in) high

Difficulty level

Beginner

Instructions

Cauliflower

Using yarn A, cast on 5 sts.
Row 1: (kf/b) to end (10 sts).
Rows 2–4: k to end.
Row 5: (k2tog) to end (5 sts).
Break yarn, thread through all sts and pull tightly. Fasten off.

Leaves

Using yarn B, cast on 16 sts.
Row 1: (p1, sl1) to end. Cast off.

To make up

Seam cauliflower and stuff. Sew leaves in place around the edge.

Tomato

Using yarn C, cast on 8 sts. Beg with a p WS row, work 2 rows in st/st.
Next row: (p2tog) to end (4 sts).
Break yarn, thread through all sts and pull tightly. Fasten off.

To make up

Using fastened-off yarn end, seam tomato. Insert cast-on yarn end inside for stuffing and work running stitch along the cast-on edge. Pull tightly to close. Using yarn D, backstitch a small cross on top for leaves.

Orange

Using yarn E, work and make up as given for tomato, omitting leaves.

Aubergine/ eggplant

Using yarn F, cast on 8 sts.
Rows 1–3: beg with a p WS row, work 3 rows in st/st.
Row 4: k1, k2tog, k2, k2tog, k1 (6 sts).
Row 5: p to end.
Break yarn, thread through all sts and pull tightly. Fasten off.

To make up

Make up as given for tomato, omitting leaves. Using yarn G, make a stalk on top of the aubergine/ eggplant by backstitching in the same spot three or four times.

Lettuce

Using yarn H, cast on 8 sts.
Row 1 (WS): p2tog, p to end (7 sts).
Row 2: k2tog, k to end (6 sts).
Row 3: p2tog, p to end (5 sts).
Row 4: kf/b, k to end (6 sts).
Row 5: pf/b, p to end (7 sts).
Row 6: kf/b, k to end (8 sts).
Rep rows 1–6 twice more.
Cast off.

To make up

Roll the piece up from one end and secure with a few stitches at the base.

Leek

Cut several 8cm (3in) long strands of yarn I. Fold in half. Beg at folded end, wrap yarn J closely around the strands of yarn until about half of the green yarn is covered. Secure yarn J with a few stitches. Separate out the unwrapped strands of

Potato sack

Using yarn K, cast on 25 sts. Beg with a k RS row, work in st/st until the piece measures 4cm (1½in).
Cast off.

To make up

Seam the short ends together, then sew the bottom of the sack closed.

Potato

Using yarn L, cast on 8 sts. Beg with a p WS row, work 4 rows in st/st. Break yarn, thread through all sts and pull tightly. Fasten off.
Note: try adjusting the number of sts and rows for variety in size.

To make up

Make up as given for tomato, omitting leaves.

Corn

Using yarn M, cast on 7 sts. Work 10 rows in g-st. Break yarn, thread through all sts and pull tightly. Fasten off.

Husks: make two

Using yarn N, cast on 4 sts.
Rows 1–4: beg with a p WS row, work 4 rows in st/st.
Row 5: k1, k2tog, k1 (3 sts).
Rows 6–8: work 3 rows in st/st.
Row 8: k2tog, k1 (2 sts).
Row 9: p2tog (1 st).
Fasten off.

To make up

Seam corn without stuffing. Sew husks together along one long edge. Place corn inside husks and secure with a few stitches.

Apple

Using yarn C, work and make up as given for tomato, omitting leaves.

VEGETABLE PATCH

Materials

For the vegetable patch:
- 5g (⅙oz) of DK (light worsted/ 8-ply) yarn in each of the following colours: beige (A), brown (B), oatmeal (C) and sandy brown (D)

For the vegetables:
- Small amounts of DK (light worsted/8-ply) yarn in orange, white, green, purple, yellow-green, red and light green
- Small amount of 4-ply (fingering) yarn in green

Size

21cm (8¼in) x 15cm (6in)

Difficulty level

Beginner

Instructions

Patch: make four

Make one each in yarns A, B, C and D. Cast on 25 sts.

Note: patch combines sections of st st and reverse st st to give textured stripes. Row 1 is a RS row.

Rows 1–3: beg with a k RS row, work 3 rows in st/st.
Rows 4–8: beg with a k WS row, work 5 rows in st/st.
Rows 9–13: beg with a k RS row, work 5 rows in st/st.
Rep rows 4–13 three more times.
Rows 44–46: beg with a k WS row, work 3 rows in st/st.
Cast off.

Side edges/middle piece: make three

Using yarn B, cast on 40 sts.
Work 8 rows in st/st.
Cast off.

To make up

Sew two patch pieces together along the longer edge. Repeat for the other two pieces. Sew the middle piece in place to connect all four patches, then attach the two side edges.

Carrot

Using orange yarn, cast on 3 sts.
Row 1: p to end.
Break yarn, thread through all sts and pull tightly. Fasten off.
Sew carrot onto the patch. Using 4-ply (fingering) yarn in green, make backstitches on the top of the carrot, leaving a long loop every other stitch. Cut loops open.

Cauliflower

Using white yarn, cast on 6 sts. Beg with a p row, work 2 rows in st/st. Break yarn, thread through all sts and pull tightly. Fasten off.
Sew cauliflower onto the patch. Using 4-ply (fingering) yarn in green, make backstitches around the flower on the patch, leaving small loops.

Broccoli

Work as given for cauliflower, using green yarn for both parts.

Turnip

Using white yarn, cast on 6 sts then break yarn.

Row 1: change to purple yarn, p to end.

Break yarn, thread through all sts and pull tightly. Fasten off.

Sew parsnip onto the patch. Using yellow-green yarn, make backstitches on the top of the parsnip, leaving small loops.

Tomatoes

Using green yarn, make backstitches onto the patch, leaving small loops. Using red yarn, work a French knot for each tomato.

Lettuce

Using yellow-green yarn, make backstitches onto the patch, leaving small loops.

Leek: make two patches

Using light green yarn for one patch and yellow-green for the other, make backstitches onto the patch, leaving a long loop every other stitch. Cut the loops open.

FIELDS WITH POND

Materials

- For the mat, use any yarn of your choice. The quantity of yarn required depends on how big you would like the mat to be. To make a 40 x 40cm (16 x 16in) mat, you will need approximately 200g (7oz) of DK (light worsted/8-ply) yarn in total. Use any yarn in your stash
- For the rocks: 10g (¼oz) of grey or light brown yarn of your choice (choose various weights and textures for variety)

Size
Rocks: 1–2cm (½–¾in) in diameter

Difficulty level
Beginner

Instructions

The mat is a patchwork of many knitted squares, making it a very relaxed project. Make squares of any size with any yarn and experiment with some new stitch patterns. This project also provides a good opportunity to practise knitting for beginners. Remember that if you use stocking stitch throughout, the edges will curl – to prevent this, use garter or moss stitch squares around the edge of the mat. Lay the squares out on a table and when you think you have made about 70 per cent of the mat, press each square with an iron, then arrange and sew them together. See how many more squares you need and in what size and make the remaining squares to fill in the space. Here are some suggestions for the squares:

Square A (vertical stripes)
Cast on 21 sts.
Row 1: k3, (p3, k3) to end.
Row 2: p3, (k3, p3) to end.
Rep rows 1 and 2 until the piece measures 8cm (3in). Cast off.

Square B (checkerboard)
Cast on 24 sts.
Rows 1–6: (k4, p4) to end.
Rows 7–12: (p4, k4) to end.
Rep rows 1–12 once more and then rows 1–6 only once more. Cast off.

Square C (double moss)

Cast on 22 sts.
Row 1: (k2, p2) to last 2 sts, k2.
Rows 2 and 3: (p2, k2) to last 2 sts, p2.
Row 4: as row 1.
Rep rows 1–4 until the piece measures 6cm (2½in). Cast off.
Cast on 22 sts.
Row 1: (k1, p1) to end.
Row 2: (p1, k1) to end.
Rep rows 1 and 2 until the piece measures 6cm (2½in). Cast off.

Square D (horizontal stripes)

Cast on 22 sts.
Rows 1 and 2: beg with a p WS row, work 2 rows in st/st.
Row 3: k to end.
Rows 4–6: beg with a k RS row, work 3 rows in st/st.
Rep rows 3–6 until the piece measures 8cm (3in). Cast off.

Square E (g-st)

Cast on 22 sts and work in g-st until the piece measures desired length.

Pond: make three

Note: change colours whenever you like – these are just suggestions.
For a two-colour pond, cast on 100 sts with yarn A.
Row 1 (RS): k to end.
Row 2: (p8, p2tog) to end (90 sts).
Row 3: p to end.
Row 4: (p7, p2tog) to end (80 sts).
Row 5: k to end.
Row 6: (k6, k2tog) to end (70 sts).
Row 7: k to end.
Row 8: (p5, p2tog) to end (60 sts).
Row 9: p to end.
Row 10: (p4, p2tog) to end (50 sts).
Row 11: change to yarn B, k to end.
Row 12: (k3, k2tog) to end (40 sts).
Row 13: k to end.
Row 14: (p2, p2tog) to end (30 sts).
Row 15: p to end.
Row 16: (p1, p2tog) to end (20 sts).
Row 17: k to end.
Row 18: p to end.
Row 19: (k2tog) to end (10 sts).
Break yarn, thread through all sts and pull tightly. Fasten off.
For a three-colour pond (two options): Change to second colour at row 5 or row 7. Then change to third colour at row 13.

Rocks

Make as many as you wish.
Cast on 8 sts. Beg with a k RS row, work 8 rows in st/st. Break yarn, thread through all sts and pull tightly. Fasten off.
You can also increase or decrease the number of stitches and rows worked to vary the rock size.

To make up

Using the fastened-off yarn end of the rock piece, sew the seam. Push in the other yarn end and close the cast-on end by working running stitch along the edge.

Sew the ponds in position on the patchwork fields. Sew the rocks around the edge of the pond.

You can fill up the little gaps around the pond with rocks or you can knit small triangular pieces by casting on a few stitches and knitting in g-st, decreasing 1 st at the beg and/or end of every row.

Add some extra texture to your mat by creating tufts of grass – backstitch in the same place several times leaving long loops, then cut the loops.

SEARCH PRESS LIMITED
The world's finest art and craft books

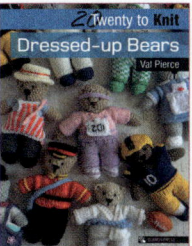

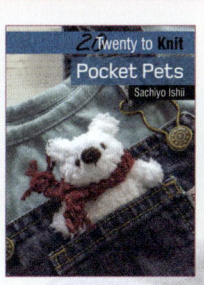

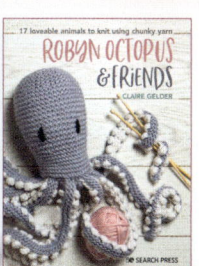

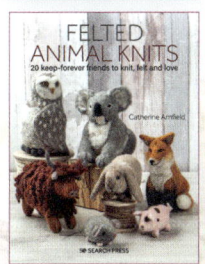

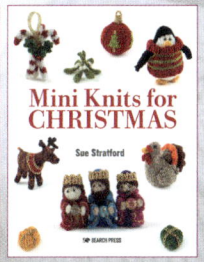

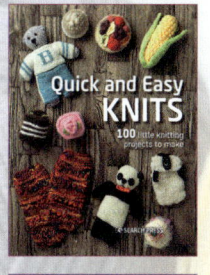

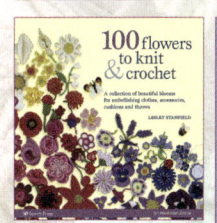

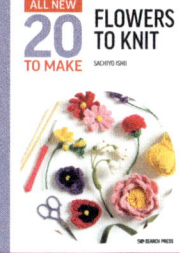

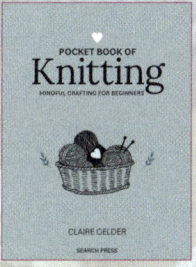

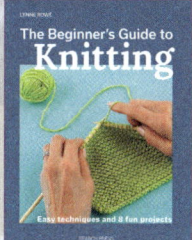

- Dressed-up Bears (Twenty to Knit) — Val Pierce
- Mini Knitted Charms (Twenty to Knit) — Sachiyo Ishii
- Pocket Pets (Twenty to Knit) — Sachiyo Ishii
- Robyn Octopus & Friends — Claire Gelder
- Felted Animal Knits — Catherine Armfield
- Bonnie the Cow & Friends — Claire Gelder
- Mini Knits for Christmas — Sue Stratford
- Quick and Easy Knits
- 100 Flowers to Knit & Crochet — Lesley Stanfield
- 20 Flowers to Knit (All New) — Sachiyo Ishii
- Pocket Book of Knitting
- The Beginner's Guide to Knitting — Lynne Rowe

For all our books and catalogues go to
www.searchpress.com

www.searchpressusa.com
www.searchpress.com.au
Please note that not all of our books are available in all markets

Follow us @searchpress on: f X P O Y

BOOKMARKED
The Creative Books Hub

from Search Press and David & Charles

WHY JOIN BOOKMARKED?

Membership of the world's leading art and craft book community

Free projects, videos and downloads

Exclusive offers, giveaways and competitions

Share your makes with the crafting world

Meet our amazing authors!

www.bookmarkedhub.com

Follow us on:
f O

@bookmarkedhub